FAITH @ SCIENCE
Why Science Needs Faith in the Twenty-First Century

FAITH@ SCIENCE

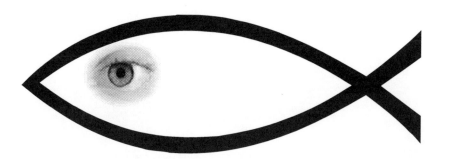

Why Science Needs Faith in the Twenty-First Century

Denyse O'Leary

Cover design by Doowah Design Inc.
Author photo by Hamish Robertson

We acknowledge the financial assistance of the Manitoba Arts Council and The Canada Council for the Arts for our publishing program.

Printed and bound in Canada.

J. Gordon Shillingford Publishing Inc.
P.O. Box 86, 905 Corydon Avenue
Winnipeg, MB R3M 3S3
Canada
ph 204/779-6967
fax 204/779-6970
jgshill@attcanada.ca

Canadian Cataloguing in Publication Data

O'Leary, Denyse
    Faith @ science:
    why science needs faith in the twenty-first century

Includes bibliographical references and index.
ISBN 1-896239-83-8

    1. Religion and science. 2. Technology—Religious aspects—
Christianity. I. Title.

BL265.T4O44 2001   261.5'5   C2001-902533-5

To Irwin Talesnick, who taught that "science is a verb."

Table of Contents

Foreword

Science was never my strong suit in school. Nor was faith, for that matter. While I am still a far cry from being an expert at either, my appreciation for the importance of each continues to grow. Science, as I see it, is primarily concerned with developing a full understanding of the material world. Faith deals with matters more ethereal. It's an easy distinction, right? In theory, perhaps.

In real life, however, science has an uncanny habit of raising the kind of thorny moral and ethical questions that people of faith are inclined to wrestle with. And recent discoveries continue to blur existing notions of the borders between physical and spiritual.

We now live in a society that is highly dependent on science and technology, a culture strongly influenced by scientific and material values. Recent scientific activity in many fields is challenging Christians today. Developments in areas such as cloning, genetic engineering, the possibility of life on Mars and environmental ethics demonstrate that any perceived separation between religious faith and empirical science is more apparent than real.

There is nothing really new in any of this. Galileo and Copernicus would attest to the fact that science and faith have been fighting turf wars for centuries. The continuing battles between creationists and evolutionists are a prime example of the belligerence and mistrust that has characterized too much of the relationship between faith and science.

This is happening in spite of the fact that people of faith have nothing to fear from legitimate scientific inquiry and the world of science has much to gain from the insights of the people of God. Many Christians are suspicious of science, but in principle we should not find it hard to believe that real science ultimately will not contradict biblical beliefs.

As the editor of a Christian newspaper, it was a delight for me to invite Denyse O'Leary to explore this fascinating engagement of faith and science. Three years and nearly 50 columns later, I have yet to hear a complaint about a shortage of subject matter. The issues of faith and science are real, but they are not insurmountable. I am grateful to Denyse for accumulating the data and presenting it in a way that even my scientifically challenged intellect can begin to get a handle on.

In my mind it is entirely possible to envision a world where good science and devout religious belief are pursued in good faith. Scientific integrity and biblical integrity are not mutually exclusive. After all, the love of God and pursuit of truth are one and the same. This book helps us to understand that science and faith will in the end prove to be allies, not enemies. We can find common ground on ultimate questions.

Doug Koop
July 2001

Preface

This book is dedicated to my Grade 12 science teacher Irwin Talesnick, who taught chemistry at Runnymede Collegiate Institute in the mid-1960s in Toronto. He believed that "science is a verb." He got rid of the lecture format and the "periodic table" memory work, and taught chemistry the way the first chemists learned—he made us do it, and then try to understand what happened and why. Another of his innovations at that school was the multiple choice exam. You could ace the exam if you observed carefully what was happening in the lab and understood the explanation. If you weren't sure how to spell sulphur (sulfur?), well, you could look it up. Issues like that were not his focus.

I don't know that the official school system ever completely accepted Talesnick's methods. But I do know two things for sure: 1) Time proved him right. The information explosion from the sciences nowadays is so immense that, as Stephen Hawking pointed out in *A Brief History of Time*, nobody memorizes and keeps up with it all. 2) He instilled, in me at any rate, a lifelong interest in the fundamental questions raised by science discoveries.

I was not able to pursue that interest, for various reasons, for over thirty years. Then Doug Koop, *Christian Week*'s editor, asked me to start writing a monthly column on science discoveries that raise issues for Christians. It was just the sort of assignment a freelance writer like me covets—I can get away with writing about practically anything in practically any science, provided it's relevant and interesting.

Thus, the book deals with questions ranging from "Is there really a Bible Code?" through "Did the Big Bang really happen?" It deals with many sobering issues too, for example, the mayhem created by anthropologists among the Yanomamo Indians, who got co-opted as the supposed demonstration model of "primitive humans," to their immense cost.

This is a collection of columns reporting on various collisions at the intersection between faith and science. It does not make any claim to be a complete map of the landscape—that would have been difficult or perhaps impossible, even for a much more learned person than I will ever be. My hope is that the book will give readers some tools, directions, and information that would not otherwise be available, perhaps to pursue these areas further than I can.

My thanks to my publisher Gordon Shillingford for his constant encouragement and timely reminders, and to the editors and designers who helped make the book possible.

Denyse O'Leary
July 2001

ONE

Moral Problems Are Not Solved by Faster Machines

At the turn of the 20th century, many thinkers were convinced that there was a "scientific" answer to all the problems that plague human existence. If only traditional religious intuitions could be turned off and scientific discoveries turned on, our problems would soon be solved.

Fast forward. At the turn of the 21st century, we have seen many valuable discoveries and many others as well. The same technology that produced the factory produced the extermination camp. The same technology that increased production threatens global environmental disaster. The same technology that enables the infertile couple to conceive enables the researcher to produce hordes of human embryos for a research project. We face greater conundrums than ever. And we may be far less well-equipped to deal with them.

The idea has arisen that machines can solve problems that their designers cannot, even moral problems. For example, Stephen Hawking, who should know better, seems to have adopted this view, discussed here in "Moral Problems Not Solved by Faster Machines."

In reality, moral problems are multiplying far beyond the ability of a civilization that tries to operate without religious beliefs. Should we permit human embryos to be cloned for various personal or industrial uses? Should we allow a large number of animal species to become extinct in order to continue a lifestyle that pleases us?

The difficulty is that, for some time, our society has tried to operate on a minimalist moral basis, suited to a machine age. We are told that an act is only wrong if it "hurts someone else." Fine, but is a human embryo or an animal species "someone else"? Is the ecosystem "someone else"? And if not, what are they?

We live in a time when the highest good promoted in secular culture is doing whatever we want. And many people stand to enrich themselves by promoting this doctrine vociferously to others. But if we operate on the basis of morally illiterate ideologies such as "total reproductive choice" or "free-market capitalism" we cannot begin to contribute useful answers to our present dilemmas. We will in fact be engulfed by them.

The columns and stories in this first group try to sketch out the general moral landscape in which we find ourselves and the nature of the problems we face, particularly in the use of biotechnology to manipulate helpless humans in the most complete and intimate ways.

Yet the odd thing is that, even as these problems are growing, events have unfolded and discoveries are made that offer great hope. We live in a finite universe where there is in fact evidence for God. We live on a finite planet where life nonetheless shows evidence of design. No matter how bleak we make things for ourselves by our own inhumanity, something always calls us back to the mystery of life in the universe. Let's investigate.

1 Big-Picture Science and Faith Find Common Ground on Ultimate Questions

At the close of the millennium, science is shoring up faith, while pushing Christians to face some very tough questions.

"Thomas Gradgrind, Sir. A man of realities. A man of facts and calculations." So Charles Dickens described his infamous 19th century materialist in *Hard Times*.

Gradgrind represented what was considered, 150 years ago, a "scientific" approach to reality: "...nothing but Facts," he insisted. As a man who embraced prevalent scientific attitudes and assumptions, Gradgrind represented a trend that would eventually declare God dead and religion absurd. Time and chance were elevated to the status of creator.

Yet when 20th century scientists started poking at Gradgrind's "Facts," his cosmos began to crumble, and it has been disintegrating steadily ever since.

Science—not Gradgrind's feared enemy, religion—obliterated his universe of atheism and materialism. Now at the close of the millennium, science is shoring up faith, while pushing Christians to face some very tough questions.

IN THE BEGINNING

Atheism is extremely plausible if you agree with Gradgrind in one simple assumption: that the universe has always existed. Even a very unlikely event such as the origin of intelligent life might happen in an infinite amount of time—because maybe anything can happen if we allow the possibility of infinite time.

If we believe that the universe (including space and time) started at a particular point, then we must ask, what sorts of events could "just happen" between then and now? And wouldn't "someone" have to start the events?

Using sophisticated instruments, today's astronomers routinely study galaxies at the outer edges of the universe, thought to be separated from us by 10 or 12 billion light years. So they have a much better picture of the cosmos than was available a century ago. Most people who study the universe no longer believe that space and time have existed forever. Rather, their studies suggest that space and time had a beginning, one that they generally place at about 15 billion years ago, in an explosive event called the Big Bang. The universe, these scientists believe, has been expanding ever since, somewhat like an inflating balloon.

A major effect of this Big Bang cosmology has been that the existence of a creator God is a reasonable assumption—not simply a matter of "faith" as opposed to "facts." God simply cannot be shoved out of any portrait of the universe that has a beginning. Even if one insists on a much briefer span of time than 15 billion years, allowing for any finite amount of time and space for the universe radically reduces the probability—which can be calculated mathematically—that the universe could form by chance alone.

But this new science poses a challenge for Christians.

Have we perhaps become too comfortable in a world where faith—so we are told—has nothing to do with science? Our Christian world is internally consistent; we seem adept at living in the arena of faith one moment and in the arena of science another, ignoring any tensions between the two. What will happen if people now say, "Okay—we see there probably is a God. What do you know about him? How do you know it? Can you prove it?"

MADE IN GOD'S IMAGE

In his cosmos without a creator, Gradgrind believed that human life is the product of an accident of self-existing atoms juggling their way through eternity. But as Michael Denton points out in *Nature's Destiny: How the Laws of Biology Reveal Purpose in the Universe*, if the universe were not organized in the precise way that it is—to many decimal places of exactitude—intelligent life (such as ourselves) could not exist.

As a result, even scientists who are not religious believers frequently come away from their studies with an overwhelming impression of design. This feature, sometimes known as the "anthropic principle," implies that God has a specific character. Apparently, he wills and purposes life. In other words, he is not just an abstraction crafted to explain how things got started, who then conveniently drops out of the equation.

Throughout the 20th century, many people have claimed that all religions are equally valid. What some often meant was that all religions were equally useless (or false or destructive), since nothing can really be known about the abstract principle called God. But if God has a character, as the anthropic principle suggests, some teachings about him must be true, and others false.

Many 20th century theologians have hoped to avoid this embarrassing and politically incorrect conclusion. They wanted to separate religion from knowable facts and defined faith in terms of virtuous feelings and commendable actions alone. They argued that religion inhabits one sphere, and science another. Religion is based on mystery, and science is based on fact. The two have nothing in common. Thus, the theologians could preserve what they really wanted to believe, safe from the glare of scientific materialism, because no one could know in a factual way what is true about God or religion. Meanwhile, some Christians retreated from science altogether, convinced that science was a synonym for atheism.

But the liberal theologians' preferred option may not really be defensible. Science is now confirming many premises that were intuited by traditional Judaism and Christianity, such as that God exists and that he planned the universe. Also, science after Albert Einstein has become more mysterious than any religion.

So, essentially, the war is over: credible religion in the 21st century must have a rational basis—but must also recognize the essential mystery of the universe, in order to do justice to what we know about God.

A COMPLEX AND MYSTERIOUS UNIVERSE

Gradgrind's resolve to stamp out imagination everywhere was steadied by his thought that he lived in a very simple, eternal universe. Like mathematician Simon Laplace (1749-1827) and many others in the 19th century, he thought that if you have enough information, the universe would be completely predictable.

In a series of discoveries so stunning that they were and still are a challenge to the imagination, 20th century science blew all that away.

Uncertainty principle: The German physicist Werner Heisenberg's Uncertainty Principle shows that one can never truly measure all aspects of the tiny particles that make up the universe. Unlike a fastball bearing down on home base, which a competent batter can hit by determining both its place and speed, subatomic particles do not have both position and speed at the same time. It would be an understatement to say this is difficult to understand, yet this bizarre but proven observation is central to making your CD player and home computer work.

It also means that the dream of a completely predictable universe and a completely planned society, much favored by atheist philosophers, is thwarted at the level of the very building blocks of the universe. A humble electron would frustrate Gradgrind indefinitely; and chaos theory—which suggests that there are vast unpredictable consequences from simple actions—would leave him devastated.

Relativity: Gradgrind believed that his watch measured eternal and infallible time, ticking away from all eternity. Space was simply the fixed distance between objects; he could measure it if he had a long enough ruler.

However, Albert Einstein (1879-1955) demonstrated considerably more imagination and insight. In addition to unleashing the power of the atom, and thereby making the equation $E = mc^2$ pop culture's only consistently recognized equation, Einstein showed that time changes with the speed at which the observer is moving. If one travels at near the speed of light, time slows down.

Meanwhile, space is not ruler-straight at all. It is curved around large heavenly bodies like our sun. (To simulate the effect, place a bowling ball on your mattress and roll a marble towards it. Will the marble run straight, curved, or both?)

These ideas are hard to understand because we can't travel the distances and speeds that make them evident. Yet phenomena such as curved space and relative time have been confirmed by scientists' observations in physics and astronomy. If ever humans do travel very far into the universe, these dynamics must be taken into account.

Quantum physics: The science that studies the behavior of the tiny quantum particles that make up atoms produced findings that were too strange even for Einstein to accept. These particles can leap great distances without actually going through the space in between. They can change their fundamental qualities to evade measurement. And light particles (photons) can behave as though time does not exist.

Niels Bohr (1885-1962), one of the founders of quantum physics, said, "If someone says that he can think about quantum physics without becoming dizzy, that shows only that he has not understood anything whatever about it."

All these discoveries leave the universe in the same condition that caused King David to muse in Psalm 139—that the "heavens" are a wonderful, mysterious place, inviting study and meditation.

Meanwhile, around the corner awaits a still more controversial issue.

SIGNS OF INTELLIGENT LIFE

When Charles Darwin (1809-1882) was working out his theory of evolution, in which all creatures descended from a single organism, he made one key assumption: that single organism was a simple jelly that might have arisen naturally through time and chance.

Yet Darwin had never seen inside a cell, the basic unit of life. That wasn't even possible until the development of the electron microscope in the 1950s.[1] When scientists peered inside, they found

21

an amazing array of interrelated molecular machines working together to perform complex functions.

In 1996 biochemist Michael J. Behe at Lehigh University in Pennsylvania stirred up a controversy with his book *Darwin's Black Box*. A Roman Catholic, Behe had accepted evolution in principle—until he tried relating it to his own discipline. The trouble was, he couldn't. He found instead that cells showed "irreducible complexity."

Many cells will not function at all unless a number of complex processes all run very precisely at the same time. Either it all functions immediately or the organism is dead. And there is no "simpler" life form that the cell could have evolved from. In fact, there is no dress rehearsal for life. This, Behe said, points to an intelligent designer behind the origin of life, rather than time and chance.

Behe's work is controversial, to say the least, among orthodox evolutionists. However, as a working biochemist his findings have been reviewed in science journals.

He said, "In private conversations a number of scientists will admit that something like intelligent design does seem to be true. [But] for a scientist to say that in public there could be repercussions. I sure wish that more of them would speak up."

It is too soon to tell whether evolution theorists will come up with an explanation or simply continue to attack Behe and others now beginning the public discussion about intelligent design. If they don't provide an evolutionary explanation, Behe's work may hammer the final nail into the coffin of Gradgrind's universe.

THE PROBLEM OF EVIL

Will these 20th century scientific discoveries make evangelism easier in the next millennium? Not necessarily.

Indeed, the scientific findings that show God's awesome handiwork actually sharpen some difficult questions, according to Hugh Ross, the Canadian-born astrophysicist who is president of Reason to Believe, a California-based evangelistic organization aimed at research scientists.

For example, when a long-awaited baby is stillborn, will the parents find it easy to believe in an intelligent designer?

"That's one of the biggest problems we have in our ministry," Ross admits. "It's not that secularists don't like what we're saying; it's that Christians don't like what we're saying. They're confronted with issues that they have never been confronted with before."

That's because a century of liberal theology has effectively separated faith from reason. Churches now expect to provide emotion-based responses to difficult issues. But if scientists begin to suggest that God exists, people are increasingly going to want churches to relate dogma to observed facts.

"When I speak on a university campus, people say, 'Okay, if [the Intelligent Designer] is the God of the Bible, I want to talk about evil and suffering, free will and predestination, the mathematical absurdity of the Trinity,'" Ross says. "These are questions that many Christians prefer never to deal with."

Ross himself loves these questions: "I've got the non-Christians exactly where I want them!" he says, "because it means that they have conceded that the traditional 'hard questions' are the truly important ones."

Phillip Johnson, a University of California, Berkeley law professor who has frequently sparred with traditional evolutionists, thinks that tackling these issues will help Christians primarily: "One of the reasons why Christianity has no intellectual standing in the universities is because it has been running away from issues," he says.

It's not that Christians do nothing. Quite the contrary; in the late 20th century, Christians have formed the backbone of palliative care, providing compassionate support for people who are dying and their families. And Christians are over-represented among people who relieve suffering, including truly difficult ministries such as in prisons and among ex-convicts. But we have largely avoided intellectual issues, thinking perhaps that we have nothing to contribute anyway. This may be about to change.

CRUSHING THE LIFE OUT OF EARTH

But, ironically, just as the world comes to accept that some of the things that we have always believed are true, our challenge as Christians has moved on to something else. Science can explain many things. But it cannot tell us what things are important. For example, it does not answer questions such as "Am I my brother's keeper?" or "What does it profit a man to gain the whole world if he loses his own soul?" or "If a man dies, will he live again?"

A more significant question today than ever before is: Will the creation itself really be liberated from its bondage to decay and brought into the glorious freedom of God? Or will it simply be progressively destroyed by human folly, until we destroy ourselves?

The biggest challenge we face today does not require an electron microscope or a space telescope. It is visible to the naked eye. It is the environmental destruction that reveals our true view of God's creation. The rapid growth of the human population during this century—based on the spread of Western science and medicine—is creating a planet on which six billion people will strive for the lifestyle of the materialistic West. But our consumer patterns, based on standards of disposability, are unsustainable.

Already, massive deforestation and the continuing global warming (probably due to use of fossil fuels) are producing profound changes in the delicate, life-sustaining physical structure of the planet. Biologists fear that the coming century will witness a great extinction in which, for example, half of all bird species alone may disappear because of forest destruction. People, as well as animals, are increasingly at risk from severe weather originating in the ecological imbalance.

Is this how we were supposed to care for creation? Or does the creation matter? Does it matter if grizzlies become extinct, as long as there are cute stuffed toys made by unschooled children in Third-World sweatshops? Is there any inherent dignity or value in, or purpose for, the people and animals that God has made, which deserves our response?

Some people—Mr. Gradgrind would understand them, no doubt—believe that cloning and other biotechnology will rescue us by preserving extinct animals in lab jars and altering our bodies so that we can withstand the growing pollution. They think the "end of nature" is a desirable thing—that parking lots are a fair trade for parks. And some Christians ask, isn't the second coming of Christ imminent and this world doomed anyway?

Noted Christian environmentalist Loren Wilkinson, a professor at Regent College in Vancouver, suggests that Christians should forget their differences about how creation got started and work to reverse the current relentless trend toward destruction. "If we're asked to stand before God in judgment and account for creation, we'll be asked to account for what we did, not what God did," he warns.

As we ponder the decisions we must now make, we should keep in mind that science originated in Judaeo-Christian and Muslim societies, among people who believed that the Earth is a good creation of God. "Science is an ally in helping us understand what creation is telling us about itself and indirectly about its maker," Wilkinson suggests.

One great irony is that in the 19th century many thinkers strenuously promoted materialism as an escape from dogmatic religion. Today materialism is a dogma from which our society needs to escape. The materialists saw science as their great ally; today science seems to be dismantling the materialistic universe block by block. Although widespread acknowledgment of the implications of what scientists are uncovering won't come easily—there will be no mass conversions or declarations of faith in the scientific community—those implications are becoming clearer all the time.

Yet great scientists are people of imagination. So are people of great faith. Once we get out from under the rubble of Gradgrind's universe, we may again see the stars—or study atoms—with heads full of knowledge and hearts full of faith, and both overwhelmed with awe.

Note: Some Christians insist on a much shorter time for the age of the universe than 15 billion years. But allowing for any finite amount of time and space for the universe, probability can help us determine if everything we discover could happen by chance alone.

2   Moral Problems Are Not Solved by Faster Machines

The likelihood of a purely technical solution to complex world problems lies somewhere between exceeding the speed of light and outrunning one's own shadow.

In early March, 1998, British cosmologist Stephen Hawking told President Bill Clinton and a gathering of noted U.S. physicists what he thought the next millennium would hold for the human race. That was a pretty ambitious project even for a man who has achieved worldwide recognition for his lifetime study of cosmic black holes. Hawking holds a math chair at Cambridge despite being so badly crippled by Amyotrophic Lateral Sclerosis (ALS) that he can speak only with the help of a computer synthesizer.

(Black holes are collapsed, lightless stars in outer space that are so dense that their gravity is infinite and all information that falls into them is thought to be lost. They are the deep space equivalent of a pack rat's "files.")

As expected, Hawking promised that a single theory that explains the forces of the universe would be developed soon. (Many scientists would rejoice at that because the two currently favored theories, relativity and quantum physics, don't work together.)

But then he got onto some other subjects, with mixed results. He opined that genetic engineers must hasten the pace of evolution by changing human beings so that we can keep up with our own scientific and technological advances.

"In a way, the human race needs to improve its mental and physical qualities if it is to deal with the increasingly complex world around it and meet new challenges like space travel. And it also needs to increase its complexity if biological systems are to keep ahead of electronic ones," he said.

Computer advances are likely to continue until the machines can match the human brain in complexity and perhaps even design new, "smarter" computers by themselves, he believes.

Now, none of these ideas is new. The really interesting aspect of Hawking's comments is the unexamined basic assumptions that he makes.

First, he assumes that greater intelligence would help us solve complex world problems. He does not try to explain why greater intelligence would help us. He just assumes that it would.

The trouble is, most world problems are not caused by a lack of intelligence. Anybody with average intelligence can see that environmental deterioration, child exploitation, abandoned land mines, and genocidal conflict are bad things, and that they lead to worse ones.

The reason that these problems are not addressed effectively is a moral one. Not enough people who have the power to do so care enough to alter their lifestyle or voting habits in order to deal with them.

Greater intelligence might help us solve problems that we are already willing to address. But it would only complicate a situation where we have made a moral choice not to address the problems. We can use greater intelligence to invent cleverer rationalizations.

Second, Hawking believes that we need to "keep up with" computers, as opposed to say, limiting their use to areas where they help us.

But one would think that North America's experience with the automobile would provide some helpful lessons here. The car took over many great cities and helped make them unlivable. The fact that the car did not destroy my own city of Toronto was largely due to a concerted effort since the 1970s to limit its inroads. We did not try to solve the problem by evolving a capacity to breathe smog.

Who knows? Our society may face the same problem with computers down the road. But if we do, the problem, again, is a moral one. What do we owe computers? What do we owe people? And what kind of a civilization do we really want? Computers are no more able than cars to take over unless we let them.

The disturbing aspect of Hawking's views is the hope that technical advances can somehow outdistance problems that are essentially moral in character. But so powerful is technological determinism in Western society that even people as gifted as Hawking tend to assume—flying in the face of all the evidence—that moral problems are merely technical problems and that they have a technical solution.

The likelihood of a purely technical solution to complex world problems lies somewhere between exceeding the speed of light and outrunning one's own shadow.

3   Genetic Engineering: Brave New World or Wild West?

When countries operate without a belief system that enables them to decide what developments are "good," they cannot direct development along any particular path.

Two recent developments in genetic engineering have raised troublesome questions about advancing human power to control and reshape the very nature of life on this planet. These questions are not purely philosophical musings.

The first development was, of course, PPL Therapeutics' much-publicized success in cloning the ewe Dolly, announced February 22, 1997. The Scottish scientists explained that they had taken the nucleus out of a sheep embryo and replaced it with the nucleus from an adult ewe's udder cell. The resultant lamb, gestated by a third ewe, was a clone that is an identical twin of the adult sheep whose udder cell was used.[2]

Scientists have cloned many species' embryos successfully. But these developments attract little attention because embryos clone (divide into twins) quite readily before they start developing specialized cells and body parts. For example, one in about 350 human births is a birth of identical twins, who are natural clones.

Dolly was front page news because the cloning of an adult animal was previously thought impossible. She opens up a world of possibilities that present-day societies, drifting without belief systems, will find difficult to manage responsibly.

Space does not permit them to be unpacked in one short article, but two issues can be noted briefly:

Most Western governments have moved to ban public funding for human cloning experiments—or ban the practice altogether. One concern is that a grief-stricken couple might try to clone cells rescued from a dying child in the hopes of "recreating" the deceased as a clone.

Anyone who has grown up in the shadow of an older sibling "hero" has experienced only a tiny twitch of the problem that the resulting child would face. As far as his parents are concerned, he has no reason to exist except to duplicate the person they have lost.

But governments cannot solve the problem of human cloning simply by banning it. Cloning will be very difficult to prevent. It employs microsurgical techniques that can be carried out at a clinic by skilled personnel, without attracting attention. And once it has been done, what are governments going to do?

The second big issue is the related subject of transgenics, the transfer of genes from one species to another. This development bore fruit in PPS's creation of "Polly," announced in July. Polly is a lamb who carries some human genes. She and four other nearly identical Polly Dorset ewe lambs are a prototype for cloned herds of sheep that produce human blood products and proteins for medical use.

Is Polly part human? That question is difficult to answer. In every life form, genes operate simply as a code. Genes are not unique to species in the way that organs or limbs are. To say that a ewe lamb has human genes simply means that she has some genetic coding that would occur naturally only in human beings.

Potatoes, snails, amoebas, sheep, and humans all use the same "codons" to convey information about body plans and operations. Codons can be cut and spliced between species and biotech corporations' stocks are soaring as they rush to be first to develop promising human-animal hybrids. PPL is currently working on pigs with human genes for heart transplants.

There are many causes for concern with these projects, but a major issue is the fact that almost all of the groundbreaking work is done in the private sector under patent. The private sector's obligation is not to fellow citizens but to shareholders. Companies have shown great unwillingness to acknowledge responsibility for environment issues. Why would they show more concern about adverse social developments from their genetic research and development, as long as their shareholders are getting a good return?

Some people wave aside all questions about these new techniques by arguing that "anything that advances medicine is good." But what if the number of beneficiaries is small compared to the number affected by undesirable developments?

When countries operate without a shared belief system that enables them to decide what developments are "good", they cannot direct development along any particular path. Early signs suggest that the 21st century will be a high biotech Wild West. It will be more important than ever for us to articulate and live by a Christian vision of life.

4   Genome Map Completion Raises Hopes, Fears

Does caring about the "human race" mean caring about individual human beings or expanding the opportunities to reject them?

Proclaiming a "historic point in the 100,000-year record of humanity," a group of scientists announced at the White House that the genetic code of human beings has been mostly deciphered. The scientists hope for cures for cancer, life extension, and other benefits. But others raise alarms about the way the process has been handled and how the information will be used.

There are two gene mapping teams, a public one led by Dr. Francis Collins, director of the National Human Genome Research Institute, and a private one, led by J. Craig Venter, the chief scientist of Celera Genomics of Rockville, Maryland. The two leaders agreed on June 26, 2000, that they had virtually completed their reading of "the book of life," the genetic information that creates and maintains human beings.

"Today...marks an historic point in the 100,000-year record of humanity," Venter informed an East Room audience. Collins told them that "We have caught a glimpse of an instruction book previously known only to God."

Practically speaking, the project is not "all zipped up with every letter identified," says Collins, predicting that the final completion will take another two years. Because the public and private efforts used different methods, the two teams will now compare their results to help search out errors and fill in gaps.

The media had highlighted the race between the two teams over the years, but Collins told them, "The only race we're interested in is the human race."

Still, Christian ethicists ask, what exactly does a statement like that mean? The White House scientists assume that "disease" is an agreed-upon concept. But in some countries, a primary use of amniocentesis is to get rid of girls. What about the potential that genome mapping creates for similar misuses?

In Canadian society, girls are not in mortal danger, but there is a lot of folklore around the "bad gene" (sometimes called the "bad seed"). Dr. Barrie de Veber, paediatrician and president of the De Veber Institute for Bioethics and Social Research (formerly the Human Life Research Institute), shared this concern with *Christian Week* as he recalled the early days of amniocentesis.

De Veber is believed to be the first doctor in Canada to do amniocentesis to assist Rh negative babies thirty-five years ago. However, the procedure started to be used far more commonly to detect and destroy babies who had Down syndrome.

Later, it was also used to detect the gene that enables cystic fibrosis. Many couples, de Veber recalls, were adamant that they wanted an abortion when their child did not have cystic fibrosis but was a carrier. The genetics team would try to reason with them, pointing out, "But you have the same gene yourself." All too often, the response was, "No, we can't have a child with a bad gene!"

Speaking of bad genes, some researchers currently claim that homosexuality, aggressive behaviour, thrill-seeking, late talking, and obesity are genetically based. Will these issues become customary reasons for abortion within the next decade?

Other issues include the fact that the gene maps of the people of Iceland (chosen because of their relative isolation from other societies) will now be sold as a commercial data base to pharmaceutical manufacturers.

Many worry about the privacy questions that ventures of this kind raise. How reliable are government claims that genetic data on an individual cannot be discovered by potential employers or insurance companies, especially when an entire database is for sale?

Thus, the key question for Christians is, does caring about the "human race" mean caring about individual human beings or expanding the opportunities to reject them?

5   Human Cloning Clinics Proposed in United States

Less than a year after the cloning of Dolly the sheep, Richard Seed, a 69-year-old Chicago area physicist, gained national media coverage and a rebuke from U.S. President Clinton after he announced that he wants to open a human cloning clinic in the greater Chicago area.

On January 6, National Public Radio reported that Seed, who has done fertility research, has been negotiating with a Chicago area clinic that owned the necessary equipment to try the procedure. He reportedly also has a medical doctor, who was unwilling to be named, who will go ahead if the American Society for Reproductive Medicine clears the proposal. Currently, the Society opposes human cloning.

Official public reaction in the United States has been swift and negative. President Clinton jumped in immediately with a statement from the White House saying that Seed's proposal was "irresponsible, unethical, and unprofessional." This was followed up by a comment in his weekly radio address that the subject was "profoundly troubling."

Clinton, who set up a Bioethics Commission on the subject last June, shortly after Dolly the sheep was announced, wants to ban human cloning research for five years because it is morally unacceptable and could undermine society's respect for life. But he has not yet been able to find a sponsor in Congress for his "Cloning Prohibition Act."

Currently, there is a ban on the use of federal funds to clone humans. The states of Connecticut, Illinois, Ohio, and Wisconsin are considering passing their own legislation against human cloning.

Seed is undeterred. He foresees developing a number of clinics in the U.S. and abroad. His initial market would be the 10 to 15% of infertile couples who cannot conceive by in vitro fertilization or by using surrogate mothers because both partners are sterile. He believes that there are 5,000 to 10,000 such couples in the United States. The child Seed produces would be an exact duplicate, a twin, in effect, of one of the parents. But he believes he will have an eventual market of 200,000 a year.

The physicist estimates that the first human clone would cost $1 million but that the cost would come down thereafter. And if the United States chooses to ban the procedure, he says he will set up in a more amenable jurisdiction such as Mexico, the Cayman Islands or the Bahamas.

Seed told ABC's *Nightline* that he is doing it for the intellectual challenge, the wish to help infertile couples, and the wish to "advance technology and to advance human civilization."

While many sources have been quick to characterize Seed as unbalanced, Clinton has several good reasons for treating Seed's proposal seriously. First, although many fertility specialists claim to oppose human cloning, they also oppose cloning bans of any kind. For example, Britain's Lord Robert Winston, who helped pioneer test-tube fertilization, called Clinton's reaction "knee-jerk" and said that cloning technology offered "hope" to many infertile couples.

Similarly, Dr. Jamie Grifo, director of the division of reproductive endocrinology at New York University, said that, while the cloning of humans was unacceptable, he was concerned that legislation might put a stop to his own experiments. He wants to try combining an egg from a younger woman with a nucleus from an older woman so that a woman who is too old to have normal eggs can have a baby anyway.

What is unclear to many observers is whether the opposition of some fertility specialists is a principled one or merely a delaying tactic until public attention is distracted by some other uproar. After all, as Seed pointed out in a recent press conference, "Science has much more experience with the human embryo than other animals," making his chances for success high. Just what that "experience" involves is something that traditionally the public has been very content not to know.

Polls taken after the announcement of the cloning of Dolly the sheep showed that 90% of Americans oppose human cloning. But Seed is not impressed. He says "I think it will take...half a dozen bouncing, baby, smiling, happy clones and their happy parents," to change their minds. Clinton, a successful politician, knows as well as Seed that most Americans who oppose cloning probably do not really know why. Thus, most of the opposition may evaporate in the wake of a sentimental news story.

In any event, Clinton also knows very well that the method Seed is using to legitimize human cloning is exactly the one that has worked so well with abortion and is presently working with euthanasia. (Just do it, claim it is a human right, get court decisions to back you, then force the defeated government to pay for it).

The American Christian Medical and Dental Society points out that cloning involves many "failures." The process of creating Dolly, for example, involved nearly 300 discard sheep, who did not make the cut due to defects at various stages before and after birth. In the case of cloning, these would be discard human beings.

The chief difficulty for Clinton is that current American and Canadian society really does not know why we should oppose human cloning. He claims that Seed is proceeding "without regard for our common values." But just what are these common values? Clinton had better figure that out soon and tell us. There may be still be time to circumvent what House Majority Leader Dick Armey calls "sidewalk cloning clinics" if the U.S. government acts quickly and decisively, although the odds are slim.

6   Don't Expect Too Much from Legislation on Human Cloning in Canada

How long will it be, I wonder, before a celebrity admits that he is cloning a child because, frankly, he prefers not to have a woman involved, except as a rental womb for his project?

According to news broadcasts in March, the federal government is once again considering a draft bill to regulate human cloning. Human cloning means producing a human being in a laboratory as an identical twin, to the customer's specification. Like Dolly the sheep.

Our government is reacting to the announcement that scientists from Italy, the United States, and Israel say they plan to clone a human being within two years.

Currently, no laws ban human cloning in Canada. That is because Jean Chretien's government has persistently failed to enact any since the early 1990s. And it probably won't really do much now.

There are several different types of human cloning proposal afloat. One is to enable a legal human being to clone an embryo (a non-legal human being in Canada) as an identical twin in order to obtain stem cells or body parts, as needed. Another proposal is to help infertile men, by enabling them to produce a clone of themselves instead of having a baby with a woman.

Insofar as there is no legal limit on the age at which a baby can be aborted in Canada, we are actually a good jurisdiction for the cloner. We're just lucky, given the way our political system functions, if we are not already a haven for biotech buccaneers.

Opponents of cloning have voiced concern recently about a Hitler-style 1930s "super-race" brought about by cloning. I think they are right to be concerned about cloning, but the eugenics argument completely misses the point. Today, governments avoid any "value" judgements whatsoever except against easy targets like Hitlerism. So they would, truthfully, plead innocent of Hitler-type plans.

Cloning today is very much a private enterprise, conducted by those who want, well, for whatever reasons, to have a clone. It is the stuff of weepy women on talk shows, not the stuff of fascists in jackboots.

The concept of "therapeutic" cloning, currently being promoted, is laughable. The reason it is laughable is that, in the absence of publicly accepted moral values, we cannot maintain a moral distinction between needs and wants.

The history of abortion legislation in Canada is significant here. The "therapeutic abortion committee" (1969-1988) brought in by Pierre Trudeau was a joke at most hospitals because killing the unborn child was never therapeutic for the child, and very rarely so for the mother.

But when medicine had embraced killing, everyone had to pretend that medicine hadn't changed at all. So doctors said that whatever the patient (now defined as the mother, exclusive of the child) happened to want was "therapeutic."

Finally, the Supreme Court stepped in and said, in a series of decisions starting in 1988, that unborn children have no rights whatsoever in Canada at any stage of gestation. Thus, the doctor can now be a little more honest—she aborts the child at any stage of gestation for whatever reason because the mother wishes it, period, and who is a doctor to judge?

And now, into a culture like this, where people would literally rather kill than judge, our government wants to introduce anti-cloning legislation?

One outcome of cloning experiments is to enable an infertile man to clone a child. How long will it be, I wonder, before a celebrity admits that he is cloning a child because, frankly, he prefers not to have a woman involved, except as a rental womb for his project? Plus, the idea of a little "him" titillates him. Why wouldn't it? After all, he is a unique and celebrated commodity. He is valuable. The child is valuable precisely because it is a clone of him.

The problem is that, to oppose cloning responsibly, Canadians would have to oppose a great deal that many currently support, for example, "total reproductive choice. " We would have to say that there are some things that should not happen in this country just because it involves reproduction, and someone really, really wants it.

Watch as the federal government tries to deal with cloning while avoiding this problem, if it does anything at all.

And this just in: from the *Toronto Sun* (March 17, 2001), we learn that an accused child molester is believed to have used a surrogate mother to breed his next intended boy victim. According to the report, he had informed the surrogate that she had to abort the child, if it was a girl.

"O, brave new world that hath such people in it." (*Tempest*, Act V Scene 1, 1 185)

7   Zapping the Gene Pool: A Last Frontier for Profits

A review of Biotechnology Unzipped: Promises & Realities
by Eric S. Grace. Toronto: Trifolium, 1997. 248 pp. $18.95 softcover

This book is highly recommended if you are a non-scientist who wants to get up to speed quickly in biotechnology. Grace provides a lucid exposition of major themes and developments in what is surely the most momentous field of scientific expansion today. One caveat: The book was written before the cloning of Dolly the sheep and does not deal with that issue except briefly in a postscript. But since biotech has come to the forefront in forestry, pollution control and medicine as well as agriculture, Dolly was the inevitable development to which *Biotechnology Unzipped* provides necessary background explanation.

Grace begins with a clear exposition of how genetics and genetic engineering work. He makes the point often obscured elsewhere that at the molecular level at which genes operate, differences between species disappear. Thus, genes from the common leech can be spliced into canola and human proteins can be grown in pigs. This opens up opportunities for commercial exploitation of Earth's creatures at a level that was hardly dreamed of fifty years ago.

Although Grace does not deal with the idea of cloning humans in any depth, he does raise the contentious issue of the patenting of human gene sequences from indigenous peoples in remote areas. He points out that this human DNA can help to treat diseases and develop vaccines. The difficulty that he does not highlight, however, is that the poor people who contributed the genetic material (under whatever understanding) will be unlikely to benefit much from any medical treatment that is developed, if it costs money. And no pharmaceutical firm is going to develop a treatment that does not cost money.

One issue that Grace does bring up is the fact that we actually know very little about most of the organisms that share the planet with us. As environments deteriorate under Western-style development, biotech methods are increasingly sought in order to shore up profitability. Manipulating the genetics of many different species for the narrow and limited purposes described in this book seems like a project similar to the devastation of large areas of the planet that is currently conducted in the name of development.

An irritating aspect of this book is the author's steadfast refusal to commit himself to a personal position on almost any issue. In many cases, his refusal assists the reader in believing that his discussion is fair and even-handed.

But he seems unwilling to commit himself to a position on the practice of American companies who are grabbing patents on traditional native medicines, depriving the traditional developers of the right to use them. He is equally silent on the question of animal suffering in the cause of high biotech.

This sort of reticence leaves the reader with a very different impression, the impression that the author assumes that "science" exists in a "value-free" realm, whereas all other endeavours are encumbered by non-scientific "values." One thing this book certainly demonstrates is that such a proposition is false. The direction of research embodies the moral attitudes and beliefs of the researchers, for which they bear individual and personal responsibility.

On some of the medical issues, Grace's own position seems clearer. He points out, for example, that the United States, where much high biotech research in medicine originates, has a relatively poor record in health care, compared to many European countries (16th in life expectancy at birth). Interestingly, while basic health care needs through much of the world go unmet, there is a big push to develop pigs engineered with human genes for transplants. And the United States, with its spotty health care record, does most of the heart transplant operations.

Grace also reveals that research at Texas A & M in the early 1990s demonstrated that universities showed the most unqualified support for high biotech, well beyond either industry or the public. One must ask therefore, whose interests really drive some of these developments? More important, what concerns have been sidelined in order to promote them?

The overall conclusion that this reader found inescapable is this: as more and more of the world is being gobbled up by special-purpose industrial and medical monocultures, ever more bizarre methods are required just to keep profits high and patch things together. The question of whether there will be a biotech apocalypse in the future seems obviated by the clear evidence that things are not working well even now.

8 Biotechnology: Canada Drops the Ball on Human Rights in Biotech Issues

For some people, the human rights of others are "fetters," limiting what they see as achievements. It is not realistic to hope for a consensus on issues like this. A society simply has to stand up for what it believes.

Recently, the Council of Europe has been working on legislation to protect human rights in an age of cloning and other biotechnology. The treaty between nations is called the Convention on Human Rights and Biomedicine, and you can find it on the Council of Europe's web site.

It's about time someone got busy on this. There are people out there who would try crossing a human being with a goat just to see if it could be done.

No doubt those people would get a prize and a patent. But what would the half-human half-goat (satyr?) get out of the deal?

Amazing as it might seem, Canada has persistently refused to pass legislation protecting human rights on biotech issues.

Our national lethargy isn't because Canadians have no idea what to do.

In the early Nineties, a Royal Commission on Reproductive Technologies headed up by Dr. Patricia Baird, a medical geneticist at the University of British Columbia, toured the country, published its findings and made recommendations. Legislation was prepared which Dr. Baird saw as a "first step."

Then the legislation died when an election was called in 1994. It was never taken up again.

This is not because Canadians are strongly divided on issues like whether it is ethical to produce half-human half-animal hybrids.

Dr. Baird told me recently that the vast majority of Canadians who addressed the Commission wanted legislation.

And it's not as if the issue isn't urgent. "We've had so many wake-up calls," she commented. "Since we reported, we had all the ads in the Toronto student newspapers offering several thousand dollars to young women to sell their eggs. We've had cloning. We've had women wanting sperm extracted from the dead bodies of their husbands ..."

Both Dr. Baird and fellow commissioner Suzanne Scorsone, Communications Director for the Roman Catholic Archdiocese of Toronto, have suggested to me that the issue was dropped because the health minister has been very busy.

I'm skeptical of that explanation. Aren't health ministers very busy in Europe? Why was the issue dropped here but not there?

Dr. Baird also suggested that there might be conflict about whether the issue is a federal or provincial jurisdiction.

Now, with all due respect to Dr. Baird, when any government in Canada wants to avoid action on any problem, all it has to do is suddenly discover that the issue is somebody else's jurisdiction.

Since we have innumerable overlapping governments in this country, some other government is easily found. And the victim government responds by assigning the responsibility elsewhere or back again.

If you don't believe me, look at the homelessness issue. For years, it seemed that the people dying in the streets were nobody's responsibility. Which meant it was all okay, right?

In this country, the question "Whose responsibility is it really?" is best answered by "Whoever can be compelled to accept it." For my (tax) money, I would rather that the federal government be compelled to accept the biotech ethics issues than a local council.

But what's the real reason why the feds haven't accepted it already?

Pressed, Dr. Baird acknowledged that the government may not want to be seen on the "wrong" side of progress in the sciences. "But it depends on how you define progress," she warned. "One can sometimes pay too great a price for progress."

Surprisingly, religious and human rights groups have generally been inactive on these issues. In the meantime, the field has been left to people with a vested financial or personal interest.

For example, Dr. Baird pointed out that medical groups like

to run their own show and do not want to be accountable to a bigger, more society-based body. And people who develop new technologies do not like to be "fettered."

The reality is that for some people, the human dignity and human rights of others are "fetters," limiting what they see as achievements. It is not realistic to hope for a consensus with them on issues like this. A society simply has to stand up for what it believes.

But whether Canada takes action or not will depend in part on whether Christians stand up for what we believe. Why is there so little interest and action on this issue?

9   Faith and Science: Why Canada Can't Act on Biotech Issues

What really prevents our government from acting on biotech issues is that it dare not appear to be too far out of step with the United States. And the United States is a "Wild West" on these issues.

My last column addressed the fact that the Canadian government has refused, for years, to pass a reasonable, middle-of-the-road bill that would provide some oversight on research that involves human beings, including human embryos. I believe that what really prevents our government from acting on biotech issues is that it dare not appear to be too far out of step with the United States. And the United States is a "Wild West" on these issues, for two reasons.

First, there is the fallout of the United States Supreme Court decision in 1973 mandating abortion on demand as an individual right. As a result, in the United States, anything to do with human embryos is now assumed to relate in some way to "individual freedom," even if the embryos in question are abandoned by their parents and grabbed by a research firm. Large pressure groups whose primary purpose is to defend abortion mount attacks against any effort to limit the use of human embryos in research.

Nigel Cameron, professor of theology and culture at Trinity Evangelical Divinity School in Illinois, told me this: "In the States it's very difficult to raise any question on its own, without having it converted into a subset of the abortion issue. Now, I think this is a disaster for North Americans because these are major questions that are quite distinct from the abortion issue, on which it is possible to find a lot of common ground with people who may take a liberal view on abortion."

By contrast, in Europe, where abortion is also legal, the abortion rate is less than half that of the United States and the Treaty on Bioethics protects human embryos from research not intended for their benefit. The difference is that the European attitude does not focus on a woman's individual right to do whatever she pleases with someone else's life, but rather on the policy benefits that are believed, perhaps wrongly, to follow from allowing some induced abortions.

Second, there is the fallout of the American attitude to human life and health care issues in general. Suzanne Scorsone, the Communications Director for the Roman Catholic Archdiocese of Toronto, who was one of the commissioners of the Canadian Royal Commission on New Reproductive Technologies, told me recently that the cultural spillover from the United States on the use of human embryos in research and other biotechnology issues "scares the socks off me."

The spillover must be seen in the larger context of a philosophy of health care to be fully understood. As Scorsone notes, the United States is quite deliberately individualistic and entrepreneurial. This makes for enormous innovation. "But it also means that when there is a problem, it is very difficult for the society to mobilize some kind of societal response," she notes.

She cites the fact that one third of the American population is not covered by health insurance, which would be an unthinkable situation in Canada, let alone in Europe. Another third is inadequately covered. One result, for example, is that while the United States initiates many high-tech advances in medicine, it also has a higher infant mortality rate than most Western countries. In other words, in a user-pay system, the high-end user may do better than the average, but the low-end user may do worse than the average. Consider what will happen if a system like that is applied to issues of human rights...

There is an ongoing debate right now about what to do with health care in Canada. Some suggest that we "privatize" the system more, along American lines. One drawback I can see is that privatization would make it even harder for us to deal as a society with major biotech issues that relate to embryo research. Sooner or later, this will include the issue of manipulating the traits of children according to parents' wishes.

In a consumer society, if people come to think of themselves as ordering children in the way that they order a new house or a new car, they are likely to take the same view: "I want what I want and I feel personally empowered to ignore the consequences that my decisions create for others!"

10   Owning Life Forms, Including Humans: Do Canadian Citizens Have a Voice?

While the Europeans are asking hard, serious questions, the servile Canadian response has mostly been gassy nonsense about the wonderful future that biotechnology promises.

In August, our Federal Court of Appeal lined up with U.S. court decisions when it ruled that Harvard University will be able to patent in Canada a genetically modified mouse that they have bred, a mouse that is prone to develop cancer.

In this ruling, the court overruled a Canadian court decision of two years ago that said that complex life forms could not be patented. The mouse has existed for a long time, and is still a mouse, even if it has been manipulated by transgenics to develop cancer easily. But now mammals can be patented in Canada.

The Canadian media coverage, which I followed, mostly promotes the line heavily funded by biotech companies, of course, that biotech firms need to own and control the world's life forms in order to stay in business and provide us all with desirable products. Indeed, one of the recommended links I followed was to a research paper by Indiana State University Phd. student Carrie F. Walter who explained that one of the reasons that a legal structure for ownership needs to be put into place is that "in addition to transgenic animals, scientists wish to patent human gene sequences and human embryos. It is therefore important that there be a solid foundation in the law of animal patents."

Imagine that! In your health care future, there may be human embryos, as human as yourself, who are actually the owned products of U.S.-based corporations, and exist only to provide spare parts or test results for those companies. These embryos may spin off into drugs or sunburn remedies for you. (The sunburn remedies, by the way, are part of an actual proposed future for human embryos, according to the U.S. biotech firm Geron.)

President Bill Clinton of the United States, as one of his first acts when he took office, changed the funding laws of his country to permit government funding of experiments in which organs are retrieved from babies aborted in the many U.S. abortion clinics that specialize in late second and third trimester abortions. Now, there are even price lists available for the arms, legs, torsos and whatnot from these hapless innocents, one of which was published last November by the *National Post*.

One of Clinton's last acts on leaving office has been to change the ruling that forbids the government to fund experiments that destroy embryos left behind in fertility clinics. The only shred of the previous ruling left is that someone other than the government-funded researcher must kill the embryo prior to the government-funded experiment.

This is a huge topic, and one column cannot unpack it. But let's start with two observations: Most members of the Canadian public have never been asked to vote on any of these momentous decisions. Have you ever been asked whether you think that a U.S. corporation should be able to own a higher life form, such as a mouse, and enforce their alleged rights in Canada? Have you ever been asked whether you think that critical portions of your health care future should depend on research done on unconsenting humans who have been deprived of human status by judge-made laws in another country or, for that matter, by judge-made laws in Canada?

Second, you can expect the current federal government to adhere closely to whatever the United States' line is, without criticism or comment. As a Canadian, I am deeply embarrassed by most of what comes out of Ottawa on these issues. While the Europeans are asking hard, serious questions, the servile Canadian response has mostly been gassy nonsense about the wonderful future that biotechnology promises. The real question, of course, is wonderful for whom? What are the true costs, as well as the true benefits? Who will pay these costs? Are they the same individuals as those who will receive the benefits? Will alternatives to the use of non-consenting humans be available? Can we even expect truthfulness from our government on these issues?

Probably the scariest suggestion about how to proceed was the one made to me recently by Patricia Baird, formerly the chair of the Royal Commission on reproductive technology issues (a commission that never went anywhere because Ottawa was unwilling to act if Clinton didn't). Baird thought that a group of elite biotech experts should get together and decide what should be done to whom. With all due respect to Dr. Baird, because I assume that she does not intend this effect, her suggestion is probably the recipe that would produce the greatest crimes against humanity. As we discovered during the 20th century, it is the elite experts who betray us. No, Dr. Baird, what we really need is a government that will permit citizens to be heard and heeded on these issues.

11 Nature in the World of "Whatever"

The buster's slogan "whatever" takes on a sharp edge when we apply it to ethics or environment issues.

Jeremy Rifkin's book, *The Biotech Century* (Tarcher Putnam New

York, 1998), provides an excellent introduction to the way in which our model of nature is shaped by our model of society. For example, he reminds us that Victorians embraced the theory of evolution because it explained and endorsed the new competitive, capitalist society. (Incidentally, 20th-century communist governments tried to sponsor alternative theories of biology precisely because they were worried by the implicit endorsement of capitalism that evolution was felt to offer!)

Now, in the same way, if we want to predict the events, outcomes, and crises of the coming biotech revolution ("getting control of the gene pool"), we must look at the understanding of life that is accepted in our society today. The people you work with and vote with assume that nature itself mirrors the society they live in. Whatever we do or would like to do in society, we can and should do to nature.

Rifkin points to the "transporter room" ("Beam me up, Scotty") in the popular entertainment vehicle *Star Trek* as a good place to begin to understand the view of human life that is gaining ground. In the transporter room, human beings are converted to energy—billions of bits of information, transferred through space by electronic pulses. They can be downloaded or not at will.

The idea behind the transporter room is that life is simply mobile information that can be altered at will without real harm. This idea started to take root about fifty years ago. For some it offered a hope of great power, for others a hope of immortality.

Rifkin quotes Gerald Jay Sussman, a professor at the Massachusetts Institute of Technology, saying, "If you can make a machine that contains the contents of your mind, then the machine is you. To hell with the rest of your physical body, it's not very interesting."

Sussman's view that mind is important and body is unimportant is not new, of course. Both Christians and Jews have condemned this view as a heresy for thousands of years, declaring that human being is not separable from bodily being. Indeed, that is why doctrines like the Incarnation and the Resurrection are fundamental to Christianity—to be a man, God had to have a body and if God defeated death, he had to regain a body.

However, the important new wrinkle on the old Gnostic heresy is that all life, including the human body, can now be conceived as a quantum of pure information, like the stuff in your word processor, to be manipulated at will. According to an increasingly popular view, natural evolution and the intrinsic patterns that it has prescribed for vast ages are coming to an end. The new evolution will be human-directed, with people reinventing themselves and changing nature, according to their current consumer needs. In other words, the planet is viewed as a sort of giant Starship Enterprise, governed by clever and well-meaning people.

Not too surprisingly, this view springs from a popular culture that denies that there are any "larger truths." As one woman explained, "truth is what is true for me today, and I might feel a different truth tomorrow, and anyway I can believe contradictory things at the same time." Try telling such a person why it would be wrong to remanufacture human embryos into sunscreen. The buster's slogan "whatever" takes on a sharp edge when we apply it to ethics or environment issues.

Now, of course, the growing environment crisis our planet faces shows that nature does have its own patterns and fragilities. Based on their current behavior, the proponents of biotech manipulations are unlikely to have worthwhile answers to these problems, because they believe that we should treat nature as a construct of our consumer desires. They deny that nature has its own realities, rules, and limits. Or, if it does, then the current nature should be replaced by a smaller, more pliable nature that they will invent.

Not too surprisingly, the environment movement emerges as one of the key competitors to the biotech movement, in offering a vision of how human power should be used. I find the vision much more promising, but there are many problems with the actual environment movement that greatly limit its effectiveness.

12 No Room in the Womb? Couples with high-risk pregnancies face the 'selective reduction' dilemma.

(Author's note: This story, which first appeared in Christianity Today, *concerns couples who found themselves in* Brave New World, *and found they could not pay its hidden price.)*

Christian couples with high-risk pregnancies, often due to biotech fertility treatments or a fetal illness, may find themselves facing an agonizing decision, not just an eagerly awaited birth.

When their physicians intensively use fertility drugs and in vitro fertilization, the chance of a multiple conception increases dramatically. In facing the complexities of gestating and birthing triplets or even octuplets, physicians often advise would-be parents to "selectively reduce" the number of living embryos in order to give the others a better chance at life. And even in the more common instance of twins, some physicians recommend aborting one of the fetuses when medical complications arise.

For Scot and Patty Shier of Los Angeles, who faced the question of selective reduction, the promise of having their own baby became a perilous journey through high-tech bioethics.

After more than four years of infertility, the Shiers sought help at a fertility clinic. Because Patty had scarring from a ruptured appendix in childhood, in vitro fertilization in which eggs and sperm are mixed in a petri dish and the resulting embryos are implanted in the womb was their only hope for having their own children.

The Shiers, members of the 2,000-member Hope Chapel in Hermosa Beach, say they prayed for God's will in the situation. But not only did several in vitro attempts fail, two adoption attempts also fell through. So they decided for one last attempt. Concerned that job stress might be part of the problem, Patty, a software support technician, took a leave of absence and waited for a call from the clinic. When the phone rang on July 4, 1995, she quickly sensed a different result. The disappointing news of a negative pregnancy test had always been administered by the clinic's sympathetic nurses. This time the doctor was on the line. Yes, she was pregnant. But the doctor did not sound happy, saying Patty should prepare for multiple births.

Twins! Patty thought. Maybe triplets. That would be a lot of work, but after all, she and Scot really wanted a family, and families are work.

The couple went for the first ultrasound examination at six weeks in utero. Nurses crowded into the room, and the doctor started counting.

One. The nurses smiled. Two. The nurses were still happy. At three, the nurses' beaming dissipated. By four, they quietly filed out of the room. At the five count, the doctor blurted, "We have to talk about selective reduction."

ROOM FOR WOMB MATES

Selective reduction, or multifetal pregnancy reduction, would mean that at around 11 weeks' gestation, a specialist would insert a needle into a fetal heart and inject potassium chloride, causing immediate death.

The stakes for multiple birth are high. There are many genuine risks for infants who have numerous womb mates, mostly resulting from premature birth. The at-risk group has a higher percentage of problems ranging from respiratory infections to cerebral palsy.

Statistically, larger women do better with higher-order multiple births, such as quintuplets. But Patty was only 5 foot 4 inches and weighed 115 pounds.

The doctor told the Shiers he did not believe in abortion, but they had no other choice. If the Shiers did not selectively reduce, the physician said, not all the babies would survive birth. Nevertheless, Patty refused to allow such a procedure. The doctor rejected the Shiers' request for a referral to a physician who would try to deliver all the babies—unless they also agreed to see two doctors who practiced selective reduction.

Scot, a stockbroker and former Air Force aeronautical engineer, worried about Patty's health. He called a Hope Chapel minister for advice. "I knew God would not want me to take a life," Scot says he decided after counseling and prayer with the pastor. "We were on the right track."

The couple never went to either reduction specialist, but made an appointment instead with a Christian perinatologist who specialized in high-risk pregnancies.

At week 8, before they visited the perinatologist, Patty lost one of the fetuses as they drove to church one night. Patty recalls having a great peace of mind despite the loss. Shortly afterward, the perinatologist started a very detailed ultrasound, identifying the offspring as Baby A, Baby B, Baby C, Baby D, and Baby E. Apparently Baby E had been an unnoticed sixth.

After that, Patty's pregnancy progressed well, which the Shiers attribute to constant prayer by their friends and other Foursquare church members. She did not require hospitalization until the twenty-seventh week. When Joshua, Jonathan, Rachel, Hannah, and Sarah came into the world on January 23, 1996, they had the best birth status to date for quintuplets in the United States. They were born at 34 weeks, with no defects, and a minimum birth weight of 3.5 pounds each. When the quints came home, 35 women from Hope Chapel acted as volunteers to help feed and care for them, and provided meals for the first six months.

IN GOD'S HANDS

Multiple pregnancies do not always end in triumph, even when biotech methods are avoided. Chad and Britta Bergacs of New Milford, New Jersey, found out in 1997 that they were expecting twins, after more than two years of trying. During an ultrasound at 17 weeks, the doctor found a tumor on one twin, whom the parents had named Joshua.

Several doctors recommended aborting Joshua to give the other twin, Matthew, a better chance. The Bergacs refused, deciding to leave it in God's hands.

Then the doctors offered another option: cesarean section, if the twins could just make it to 28 weeks without complications.

Afterward, surgeons said, they could operate on Joshua and remove the tumor. Britta agreed to partial bed rest, living with her in-laws so she could receive treatment in Philadelphia. But by 28 weeks, Joshua began to show the effects of his tumor. The night before the operation, both twins died. "My husband and I were devastated," Britta recalls. "But, we have never thought twice about giving both our boys a chance. We don't have to explain to a remaining son why we aborted his brother." The Bergacs have joined the waiting list for an adoptive child.

Doctors also told Robert and Nicole Klan of Bethel Park, Pennsylvania, to "reduce" their triplets, two boys and a girl. The advice is routinely dispensed at just over five weeks, when a fertility-drug pregnancy is confirmed—but before there is any indication of medical complications.

The Klans, who are Baptists, turned down the initial advice, but doctors renewed the appeal at 17 weeks when an ultrasound showed that the two boys had defects. An amniocentesis test suggested that only one of the boys had a defect—spina bifida.

After agonizing for several days, the parents refused to "reduce" him. "Eventually we realized that God did not make mistakes," Nicole recalls. "He would work it out for our good and his glory." When Trisha, Jonathan, and Jaden were born in September 1997, Jaden had no mobility from the hips down. In August, the triplets celebrated their second birthday. Jaden gets around by using arm braces, which his mother considers a miracle.

IS BIOTECH AN OPTION?

Is high-tech fertility a legitimate option for Christians? Gilbert Meilaender, professor of Christian ethics at Valparaiso University, thinks not. "Parents, including Christian parents, need to get a grip on this overwhelming desire to have their own child. If this is what it takes, then that desire should be repressed," he says.

Meilaender is troubled by the tendency for children to become the products of a process and for parents to become victims when things go wrong with the process. "But the real victims are the children, who are often born with considerable defects or get fetally reduced," he says. "It's all too easy to think [as a parent] that, because I have to agonize over this, I am the one who is being victimized."

But William Dodds, a Christian Reformed physician who practices at Michigan Reproductive and In Vitro Fertilization Center in Grand Rapids, Michigan, disagrees. "I think it is important for Christian physicians to be involved with reproductive medicine," he says. "Christians can help shape what should be done. Christians can help couples make decisions that are in concert with Christian principles."

Dodds also believes that it is possible to perform assisted reproductive techniques in a Christian manner with a very high respect for human life. "I see these as just techniques," he says. "In and of themselves, I don't think they're wrong."

Dodds opposes research on embryos and discarding embryos. "Our principles are that once an egg is fertilized it is a human life and respected as such," he contends. While he is legally required to tell couples of their right to selectively abort children in higher-order pregnancies, he does not advise them to do so.

He also feels that the risk of multiple births is actually greater with fertility drugs, in which the number of eggs released may be unpredictable, than with in vitro fertilization, in which the number of embryos implanted at a given time can be controlled.

But fertility is big business. The reputation of clinics depends on "success rates," says Gene Rudd, a former obstetrician-gynecologist who is associate director of the Christian Medical and Dental Society.

To enhance their standing, Rudd says, clinics use techniques that increase the risk of multiple births, and then often offer the couple selective reduction if a large number of embryos are successfully implanted. According to Rudd, 75 percent of all multiple gestations in the United States today are due to high-tech techniques: 35 percent to in vitro fertilizations and 40 percent to fertility drugs.

"In in vitro fertilization, they take lots of eggs, fertilize them all, and take four, five or six and implant them, knowing that their success rate is higher," he says. In the high-tech reproductive world, one embryo has a 12 to 15 percent success rate. Four embryos give a 50 percent chance of one live baby.

When clinics compete for money and success rates, they are pressured toward fertilizing and implanting more embryos, Rudd says. Clinics view a live birth of twins as a score of two, even if the twins started out as quintuplets—so long as the parents accept reduction.

What if patients tell a clinic that they only want to fertilize and implant two or three eggs, because they did not think they could handle an instant family of four or five? "There's the rub," Rudd says. "Clinics don't want to do that. They would do it if the couple insisted. But often, they don't offer that alternative to patients."

Joe McIlhaney, president of the Austin, Texas-based Medical Institute for Sexual Health, says both patients and physicians often insist on going ahead because the patients who turn to advanced reproductive technology have typically gone through years of infertility. "There's a sense of 'Anything we can do to get pregnant is worth it,'" he says.

It is the same story with fertility drugs such as Metrodin and Pergonal. McIlhaney, an obstetrician-gynecologist for 28 years, bluntly states that most of the multiple pregnancies "don't need to happen." He suggests that a doctor should monitor egg follicles that ripen and skip cycles when fertility drugs have caused large numbers to ripen at once (the condition necessary for multiple babies to be conceived).

Christian couples need to realize that avoiding ethical dilemmas may take a little longer, cost more, and involve additional discomfort, says William Cutrer, an obstetrician-gynecologist and associate professor of Christian ministries at Southern Seminary in Louisville, Kentucky.

Cutrer believes that couples should refuse to implant any embryo they do not expect to carry to term. He also recommends against having embryos frozen in liquid nitrogen, in case future attempts are needed. What will be done with ten frozen embryos if the couple has already had triplets?

"If you only fertilize three eggs a cycle, you don't have ten more in the freezer to try next month," he says. "You have to go and reharvest eggs, so that would be expensive. But you avoid the ethical quagmire." He doubts that a couple's chances of taking home at least one baby are harmed by ethical caution.

There are now about 100,000 human embryos in liquid nitrogen tanks around the United States, McIlhaney says. Generally, they are discarded after five years. There is increasing pressure to use them for research, although some are exploring embryo adoptions (see "Snowflakes," below).

WHO IS IN CONTROL?

Women who have struggled for years with infertility have trouble picturing themselves with even one child, let alone a large, instant family. Looking back, Nicole Klan recalls that she never really anticipated triplets, although multiple births are listed as a possibility on fertility drug labels.

And Scot Shier, father of quintuplets, was assured by the fertility doctor that the Shiers would be fortunate if one of their six or more in vitro embryos actually made it to birth.

Even without modern interventions, older women are more likely to have multiple births than younger women, Rudd says. And now, when more women delay pregnancy until middle age and seek assisted reproduction, the numbers rise.

But will a Christian couple have the opportunity to follow an ethical approach? Louise Bijesse of Stony Brook, New York, was shocked when her obstetrician suggested reduction of her triplets, who were healthy and born without any disabilities last year.

Individual Christians and churches provide lots of support and moral advice, but referrals to Christian medical help and awareness of specific risks lag far behind.

For example, the Christian Medical and Dental Society does not provide a list of fertility clinics that follow Christian principles, because it has no way of ensuring professional competence.

Cutrer does not feel it is necessary for Christians to seek out Christian doctors or clinics. "That's not as important as knowing what the procedures are and what you believe. The clinics will generally work with the patient. They couldn't care less about the Christian ethical point of view, but they are willing to limit the number of eggs that are exposed to sperm, limit the number that are reimplanted, so the patient really can control that aspect of care."

Clergy usually do not know the ethical dilemmas that Christian couples risk, says Robert Evans, president of the California-based Veritas Christian Research Ministries, which provides bioethics seminars in churches. Too often, he says, counseling focuses on the issue of whether couples should pursue assisted reproduction at all and ignores critical details.

But does the problem lie in the critical details or in a critical shift in thinking? Meilaender, for example, is skeptical of efforts to set up the procedures in order to avoid selective reduction. He believes that, while such efforts are well meant, they may miss the point of the problem. "The very fact that we have this technology helps all of us to think of children as our personal project," Meilaender says. "I think we don't even realize how much the Christian community has bought a general attitude toward having children."

LINGERING DOUBTS

Those Christians who opt for selective reduction do not seem to find it the easy way out. One woman, identified only as "Rebekah," posted a message to Hannah's Prayer, a Web-based resource for Christian couples struggling with infertility (www.hannah.org). Faced with a move overseas, she opted to have her triplets reduced to twins and now longs for her "little lost triplet."

"I pray that I will be forgiven by God and would like to get the word out to anyone who is considering selective reduction that scars left by such a procedure last far longer than a difficult pregnancy," she writes.

Theresa Burke, founder of Rachel's Vineyard, which conducts post-abortion retreats, remembers a couple pressured by doctors to reduce their quadruplets to twins and then experienced much grief and guilt.

Infertile couples are especially fragile, she says. "They value the life and they've struggled to conceive. So when a child is created because of all their efforts, they want to keep them." Her retreat enabled the couple to name their lost babies and grieve for them.

Despite their high-tech story, now that the quints are three years old, the Shiers behave like any traditional large family: They buy economy sizes, and Scot proudly hails his wife as the queen of garage-sale shopping. "She never pays more than a dollar for their clothes," he says.

Patty often thinks about their sixth baby. "I will look around and all five children will be with me, and I think one of them is missing. In a sense, one of them is missing." She has thought about the pressure she faced for selective reduction: "I wish that we had done a better job of investigating clinics. There's got to be Christian fertility doctors out there. There just have to be."

SNOWflAKES EMBRYO ADOPTION: A NEW SERVICE MATCHES DONORS AND WOULD-BE PARENTS.

Barbara Olson, 36, and her husband Dan, 39, of Minneapolis were content with the size of their family. The Olsons had two children through in vitro fertilization but were concerned about what to do with their leftover fertilized eggs.

The fertility clinic had provided the Olsons with two options for the extra embryos: freeze or dispose. Not wanting to end the potential for life, the couple opted to place the nine embryos in straws in the clinic's deep freeze.

"I was distressed over the fact that our embryos were just in storage and I felt convicted that they deserved a chance to be born," Barbara says.

Then the Olsons learned of the Snowflake Embryo Adoption Program. Ron Stoddart and Christian Adoption and Family Services (CAFS) in Brea, California, launched the one-of-a-kind program, which uses traditional adoption methods to find homes for abandoned embryos, two years ago.

Stoddart says the name Snowflake is appropriate because embryos are "unique, they're fragile, and of course, they're frozen."

The first Snowflake baby was born to a California couple in December 1998. Snowflake has matched three sets of couples so far, and is working on five more. The agency has a unique ministry opportunity: there may be as many as 100,000 surplus human embryos frozen in fertility clinics across the country.

While fertility clinics often provide donor embryos to those who request them, Snowflake requires a traditional adoption home study and asks that the parents of the frozen embryos select the adoptive couple from qualified applicants.

Because the embryos have no legal rights, the agreement is not a legal adoption but a transfer of property.

Some fertility clinics do not want to handle adoptions, but welcome the opportunity to turn over a donor program to an experienced adoption agency, says JoAnn Davidson of CAFS. The price for embryo adoptions, between $7,500 and $10,000, is similar to other adoptions, Davidson says. This amount includes estimated legal costs and Snowflake's $3,500 fee for a home study. Neither the donor couple nor the fertility clinic receives any of the adoption payment.

The initial fee does not come with a motherhood guarantee. Since pregnancy can be difficult to achieve on the first try, the adoptive couple receives at least nine embryos, enough for six to seven cycles. Unused embryos are matched with another couple. But if an adoptive couple uses all of a donor couple's embryos and still has not become pregnant, matching with another couple costs an additional $500.

The uncertain fate of surplus frozen human embryos has become the subject of sharp political debate in Congress. Some biotech researchers hope to use excess human embryos for experiments that would be lethal to the embryo but may enable medical advances.

After contacting Snowflake earlier this year, the Olsons were matched with a couple in Georgia. After months of phone and e-mail correspondence, the adoptive couple flew to Minneapolis in October to meet the Olsons and receive the embryos. They expect a pregnancy this year.

TWO

How Big Are Our Footprints?

The looming environment crisis is easier to understand if we consider the example of a family in charge card debt. The debt starts out small. It is easily carried. After a while, it is less easily carried. Then it becomes hard to carry, even though the family starts to economize. Finally, the debt takes over and bankruptcy looms.

Unfortunately, as bank managers can testify, by the time the family realizes that they are tipping towards bankruptcy, they are often quarrelling, blaming each other, and separating. John refuses to economize on pizza because Jane bought a video. And daughter Carla shows them both by treating herself to a Gucci scarf. Rapid acceleration downhill.

The similarities are obvious. Canadians blame Americans for pollution and Americans export the blame right back to us. We blame Third World nations for rapid population growth and then point with pride to rapid motor vehicle growth as evidence of our success as a society. Everyone rationalizes his own contributions to the problem and confesses the sins of everyone else.

Corporate public relations around environmental issues becomes a growth industry, but may represent no real change. After all, the environment is not an asset on anybody's balance sheet. Pollution is not an expense on income statements.

Meanwhile, high-level warning indicators, including the collapse of fishing industries, show that just keeping environment issues off the corporate agenda is not really working. So the next dodge is biotechnology. When pollution levels are not sustainable in nature, we will manipulate life forms to create new ones that find the level sustainable. If species become extinct as a result of our activities, we will clone them and keep them in biolibraries, in case the day ever comes that we need them for something.

Historically, people who do not face up to realities face crises instead. So there is little doubt about how all this will end.

But two problems face Christians who want to take environmental responsibilities seriously: First, how can we change our lifestyles? And second, how can we make a difference if our neighbors are still into rationalization?

The most helpful response to the first question, in my view, is offered by Professor William E. Rees, who teaches at the School of Community and Regional Planning at the University of British Columbia. He suggests looking at one's individual "footprint" on the earth. By that, he means the amount of the earth's productive resources required to sustain a person. Thus, the energy required to heat your home and drive your car, as well as to feed, clothe, and entertain you, must be factored in.

The advantage of Rees's approach is that it circumvents the "blame circus" by asking for a total inventory. In other words, working towards a responsible attitude to the environment means reducing our overall total, not quarreling among ourselves about the legitimacy of the subtotals. The principle, clearly, is the same as a family budget. Assigning ourselves a total leaves room for personal choice within a framework at the same time as it asks for overall accountability.

As to the second question, does what we do individually make any difference? I don't know. But here is what I do know: people never ask that question about the things they really care about.

Does the father fulfilling a prescription for his child's illness hesitate, wondering if the medicine will really make a difference? Does the school bus operator who is told that her brakes are faulty hesitate, wondering if she can get away with driving kids home on mulched brakes? Does the homeowner whose basement is full of methane gas just hope that the problem won't become too serious?

We would hope not. All these people should want to be sure that they did everything they individually could in order to make a difference. Even if the solution to a problem is costly, they should know that they have to address it.

For too long, environmental issues have been the sort of thing we vaguely hoped that government or funky new inventions would take care of. But it isn't happening like that, as the Walkerton water crisis brought home so devastatingly to a small town in Ontario last year. The following selection of columns and articles is presented as a challenge to think carefully about the environmental consequences of the decisions we make.

13   Are Christians Implicated in Environment Destruction?

Once we accept that looking for scapegoats is not a solution, we must ask ourselves what we can do personally and as Christian communities to make a difference.

Anyone who looks at recent statistics on the rate of environment destruction on this planet will want to just turn away their face. Over the next half century, forest destruction will doom about half of all bird species, according to experts. Even conservative estimates suggest that large percentages of plants and animals will simply disappear.

In the last thirty years, probably in response to the need for scapegoats on the environment, the idea has grown up that somehow Christianity is the cause of environment destruction. The idea that Adam and Eve have some special responsibility to look after creation was said to justify the destruction.

Of course, on the face of it, this is nonsense. Quite obviously, if we believe that God will judge us for destroying the environment, we Christians should be more vigilant than most people.

Even more silly is the idea that if we would just get it through our heads that human beings are merely an overbred animal species, we will be more motivated to do something about the global environment problem. Why would we? If we really believe that we are just clever animals, why would we do anything more than fight viciously among ourselves for survival? That is what animals do when their environment comes under stress.

No, we must start by believing that reason and moral choice are true categories of human behaviour and that we in particular have a special responsibility to act. Otherwise, we will not find the strength to re-evaluate our lifestyle choices and make the necessary changes, nor will we earn the trust of Third World citizens to work with us. Trust between nations will be fundamental to a solution.

WHY AREN'T WE DOING MORE?

But the significant question that the accusation raises is, why aren't we doing that right now? Why are so few Christians concerned and involved in the environment issues which become more pressing every day?

Here is my view, for what it is worth: we have become badly compromised worshipers of Western consumerism. Remember that traditionally, Christianity was an ascetic religion. Christians were taught to consider material possessions and personal comforts to be of little account compared with eternal life. As Thomas à Kempis put it in *The Imitation of Christ*, "Behold, the wealthy of this world shall consume away like smoke: and there shall be no memory of their past joys."

One practical problem with Kempis's point of view is that while some people moderate their desires in order to attain the Kingdom of Heaven, others are poor because of social injustice. Spiritually, neither they nor their oppressors benefit.

Our response in the Western (and largely nominal Christian) world has been to try to solve the problem by supporting the growth of technology. The export of technology raised living standards around the world. Many peoples adopted and further developed the technology. Indeed, Christians have been in the forefront of exporting the benefits of clean water, health care and education to remote areas. But unfortunately, the effect of that vastly increased human activity on the natural world was completely ignored and the devastating results are now coming in.

Once we accept that looking for scapegoats is not a solution, we must ask ourselves what we can do personally and as Christian communities to make a difference. First, we must repent. As Western Christians, we were hypocritically delighted that new technology enabled the human "pie" to grow so that we could increase our own consumption while still sparing merely a small slice for poor neighbors. In other words, we appeared generous in our own eyes while making few real sacrifices. We refused to see that the pie was growing at the expense of the health of the entire planet's ecosystem.

That approach to the Christian life cannot continue. We Western Christians in particular should reclaim the traditional idea of moderating our desires and living simply, so that we are not an inevitable source of continued destruction. Certainly, we cannot hope to convince poorer countries that they ought to care about the environment while we ourselves fuel the demand for environmentally destructive practices in those very countries by our own habits of consumption.

But slowly Christians are starting to move in this area. For example, St. John's Shaughnessy, an evangelical Anglican church in Vancouver, is hosting a Visions for the Earth environment conference in April, 1989, sponsored by Vision TV. Let's hope the conference generates practical suggestions for making a difference while there is still time.

14   How Big Are Our Footprints?

How many of us know what happens to the things we throw away? Do they simply disappear somehow? Or do they live on to poison rivers and disfigure landscapes?

Are our footprints on the earth tiny, shapely prints, easily erased by the water, the wind, and the sun?

Or are they deep bulldozer ruts that create permanent,

widening pools in a fragile landscape, spelling doom for a multitude of God's creatures?

Sadly, because of the environment degradation that supports our throwaway society, we Western women may be more bulldozer than Cinderella.

Professor William E. Rees, who teaches at the School of Community and Regional Planning at the University of British Columbia, suggests that we look at our environmental impact in this way: the amount of land on the surface of the earth that is required to support each of us, given our actual habits, is our footprint on Creation.

If we require a lot of land to support us because of rampant consumerism, we have a much bigger and more permanent footprint than if we reduce, reuse, and recycle.

Modern technology has brought many blessings. But the blessings have not been shared by the whole Creation. Wholesale devastation of natural landscapes are beginning to take their toll on the planet, as a multitude of recent news stories show.

Global warming, for example, is either caused or exacerbated by the constantly increasing burning of fossil fuels (coal, oil, and gas). So many animal and plant species are becoming extinct that biologists now speak of this era as a Great Extinction.

Over the next half century, forest destruction will doom about half of all bird species, according to experts. One in eight plant species is expected to simply disappear.

Is this how God intended us to care for Creation?

Books have been written explaining what is happening in environment issues. But here it is in a nutshell: most of the six billion human beings in the world today want Western standards of living. Who can blame them? We live very comfortably compared to most people. But if everybody does what we have done, the planet will be destroyed over the next century by the combined pressures of global warming and environmental pollution.

The only solution is to stop doing what we are doing, before attempting to convince others that they should not imitate us.

However, the good news is that there is still time for Christians to make a difference. We need to start by recovering some important elements in our faith, principally the sense that we are the stewards of Creation, not merely consumers of it.

For example, how many of us know what happens to the things we throw away? Do they simply disappear somehow? Or do they live on to poison rivers and disfigure landscapes? Do we even ask these questions? We had better start asking, because the answers are becoming very important.

In truth, we Western Christians have been badly compromised by materialism. Consider, for example, what a Hindu mystic who embraced Christianity had to say after visiting our culture early in this century:

> While sitting on the bank of a river one day, I picked up a solid round stone from the water and broke it open. It was perfectly dry in spite of the fact that it had been immersed in water for centuries. The same is true of many people in the Western world. For centuries they have been surrounded by Christianity; they live immersed in the waters of its benefits. And yet it has not penetrated their hearts; they do not love it. The fault is not in Christianity, but in men's hearts, which have been hardened by materialism and intellectualism...
> (Sadhu Sundar Singh, 1889-1929)

To help the Creation recover from environment damage, we need to renounce materialism and the throwaway society, and regain our sense of stewardship. But as we work on this goal, we must not be seduced by mere legalism and the crippling guilt that goes with it. By promulgating rules without support, legalism frustrates our good intentions and accomplishes nothing for Creation.

For example, if we all use our cars less we will be making a big contribution right away to reducing greenhouse gas emissions. But reducing the use of our cars is practical only where public transit systems are clean, safe, and convenient.

Christian women can make a difference by lobbying for better public transit. But we will have no impact if we merely feel legalistically guilty about driving, but drive anyway because we know that local public transit is too poor to be a reasonable choice.

Again, churches can help by using china cups rather than plastic foam disposables. But this change may be resisted if it means that a few stalwart saints have to spend hours washing up after every main service. A large church should install a commercial dishwasher so that reusable china cups mean a sustainable environment, not martyrdom for a faithful few.

There are many practical ways we can make a difference, though each of them requires research and involvement in our communities. For example, a current campaign by the Toronto Transit Commission addresses the fact that Revenue Canada rules state that employers are not allowed to buy transit passes for employees as a non-taxable benefit. But employers are allowed to provide on-site parking as a non-taxable benefit. Clearly, this situation encourages the use of private cars, even in cities like Toronto that have comprehensive transit and severe traffic congestion problems.

As Christians, we must become more aware of the many legislative and economic barriers to responsible choices in these areas and provide support for environmentally responsible public policies.

But perhaps our most difficult mission will be to challenge the materialism that just "sort of happens" in our lives because the secular culture endorses it—shopping as a recreation, for example. As Christians, with a responsibility for Creation, we need to ask not only what happens to the things we throw away, but what is the real cost to the Creation of the new things we acquire? Do they expand the size of our already huge footprints?

Fortunately, as business and government are becoming more aware of environmental issues, they are offering more environment-friendly choices. For example, your church may be able to buy recycled (and recyclable) paper, coffee grown in sustainable forests, and other "fair trade" products that offer Third World farmers a fair price, thus reducing the need for practices that are unfriendly to their environment.

But perhaps, best of all, twinning with a Third World church will help put our priorities in perspective. When we are praying with fellow Christians who struggle to pay their children's school uniform fees and vaccination costs, we will know better how to view the mindless materialism that infests our own culture and prevents us from seeing our vocation to care for Creation as Christians more clearly.

15 More Money Will Not Make You Happier, Prof Claims

Free-market arguments on environmental issues do not take into account the fact that the climate and the environment have never been on the balance sheet. They have never been anybody's responsibility to protect and no one is consistently doing it.

Would you be just as happy with a much lower income? Recent research suggests that you might.

Now, relax. Your boss is probably not reading this. Even if he is, solve the problem by showing this article to *his* boss. That will prevent your immediate boss from warping out on the blissful possibilities of a low-income paradise for you—but not, of course, for him.

Professor William E. Rees, who teaches at the School of Community and Regional Planning at the University of British Columbia, told the annual meeting of the American Association for the Advancement of Science in Anaheim last month that the main benchmarks of human well-being literacy, longevity, and low infant mortality only increase up to about $7,500 international dollars per person per year.

As incomes increase beyond those levels, no further objective improvement occurs in health and welfare. The gains represent increasing consumption which, Rees says, contributes to escalating, dangerous climate change without improving human welfare.

Even more surprising, there is not much subjective improvement either. "If you undertake international surveys of how people feel about themselves (as in "Am I happy—on a scale of one to 10?") little difference emerges between people whose per capita income is $10,000 versus people whose per capita income is $20,000," he explains.

He concedes, however, that income disparities that are perceived locally as unfair do create intense unhappiness.

Professor Rees, who thinks that rich countries should power down consumption to save the planet, has taken a lot of heat recently for his views. John Barber, a *Globe and Mail* columnist, accused that, "In the name of saving the planet, a bunch of rich people in rich cities in the world's most highly urbanized countries now want to stop others from sharing their good fortune."

The *Globe* also devoted an editorial to slamming Rees as a "professionally purse-lipped ascetic" claiming that his views are "a recipe for stagnation." (January 29, 1999).

Professor Rees struck back at his critics in a recent interview with me, accusing the Globe of "going bananas" and making a collective "ass" of itself, ignoring the critical issues of global deforestation and climate change that the business world is slowly coming to terms with.

Even the traditionally conservative insurance industry is running for cover, he notes, in the face of climate change, much of which can be traced to human activity.

From my experience, he's right. Munich Re, the world's largest reinsurance company, has gone on record as saying that, comparing the figures for the 1960s with those from 1987-1997, the number of major natural catastrophes was three times larger and cost the world's economies, after adjusting for inflation, eight times as much. The company blamed climate change related to global warming and greenhouse gas emissions.

Professor Rees, who has coined the term "ecological footprint," says that the human footprint on the earth is no longer a fragile mark, largely erased by the sands of time. Because of the sheer numbers of human beings who all want current Western standards of living, it is now more like Godzilla's wake, stamping out thousands of plant and animal species and altering climate patterns by producing vast deserts.

Professor Rees's "ecological footprint" works like this: the amount of the earth's productive resources required to sustain you, no matter where you live, is your "footprint" on the earth. Thus, the energy required to heat your home and drive your car, as well as to feed, clothe, and entertain you, must be factored in.

His critics, including Mr. Barber, argue that environmental problems can be solved by innovation and that higher standards of living are the best recipe to produce more environmentalists.

But Professor Rees thinks that free-market arguments do not take into account the fact that the climate and the environment have never been on the balance sheet. They are viewed, like the Canadian forests and coastal fisheries, as a "free service of nature." They have never been anybody's responsibility to protect and no one is consistently doing it.

Hence, he hopes that people in rich countries like Canada can learn to be happy with smaller feet and a shoe size somewhat closer to Fay Wray's than Godzilla's.

I think we Christians better go back to Genesis and grasp the fact that we are looking after this planet for Somebody Else, not just exploiting it for whatever we happen to want. That will help us decide what we should do and accept.

16 Genetically Engineered Foods: Is the Future of Food Back in the Past?

It's about 8:00 o'clock on a cold Saturday morning in January at a winery that owns a big cold room in Toronto. The winery's own business for the day hasn't actually started yet. Still, I am not the first one there by any means.

The largely non-English-speaking crowd uses "sort-of-English" as a lingua franca, but no one cares about the fine points of grammar. Here, the only language that matters concerns the basic stuff of life: food.

Lucky people like me, for whom neatly hand-lettered invoices can be found, proceed to a desk where they can fill their advance orders for cheeses, eggs, honey, syrup, huge free-range chickens, sausages, and meats. The ones for whom invoices cannot be found can buy whatever "extra" meat, dairy produce, honey, and syrup the Amish and Mennonites who farm outside Toronto can make available to them.

The crowd grows as the morning progresses. I am very lucky I got in and out early because, as in any old-fashioned market, the finest chicken sells the soonest. Mine looks pretty good.

Is this an imagined scene from the year 1800? 1900? Nope, it happened last Saturday in 2000, just north of Pape and Danforth.

Fortunately, I ordered by the Internet, so my invoice was processed early and the clerk found it almost immediately. The produce is a little more expensive than what I could buy at the supermarket. But no one, not even the poor immigrants who are trying to locate their invoices behind me, seems to care.

The flavour is wonderful. But more important, everyone here is drawn by the same promise that drew me: no hormones, no antibiotics, no pesticides.

No one even mentions genetically altered foods (creatures with animal and plant genes spliced together to produce odd, commercially useful effects). If anyone here knows about them, they take for granted that the people who brought us the miracle of affordable, chemical-free food can easily manage to stay clear of what Europeans call "Frankenfoods."

I am going to take a couple of columns to talk about the increasingly contentious issue of genetically altered foods. But first, I thought it was fair to begin by revealing my bias on this subject: I am one of the increasing number of Canadians who already go out of our way to avoid the interventions that are now taken for granted in supermarket foods.

I did not used to be this way. But two years ago, a sister who has lost about three or four years of her life to migraine headaches asked me to look at a book she acquired through the Internet (that much-deprecated source of electronic medical quackery). The doctor who wrote the book suggested that women who suffer severely from migraine headaches may have too much estrogen in their systems. He also suggested that this problem may be increased by the fact that many farm animals are given estrogen to increase their productivity.

I, who have lost about a year of my life to migraine headaches, responded, "Well, I don't know. But why not just try all-natural foods? If it works, we don't even need to know exactly why!" So we located sources, and carried out our plan.

Since then, I have lost only one day to migraines in the last six months because I was eating in a restaurant on a day away from home. My sister has also experienced significant respites, as long as she is able to stick with the Amish and the organic food.

But we are only two, related people, not a research study. When I mentioned our adventures to a physician friend, I expected him to say we were crazy. Instead, all he said was this: No one with a big budget to promote something high-tech is going to tell us to just go do what the Amish do. But we may as well continue if it works. And we have.

I guess, in a world dominated by the public relations firms of big companies, there are some things you figure out for yourself if they are important enough to you. I just wish that my sister and I had had any inkling of possible solutions back in the decades when we were told that migraines are "caused by stress."

17 Should You Know What You Are Eating? Government Says No; Christian Farmers Say Yes

The Canadian government thinks you don't need to know if you are eating genetically modified foods. Many Christian farmers disagree.

Tomatoes with fish genes? The biotech industry is currently working on splicing fish genes into the tomatoes you eat, to give them a longer shelf life in the supermarket. They claim it is nothing new or worrisome—people have been crossbreeding vegetables for thousands of years.

Um, er, yes, but we haven't been crossbreeding them with

fish. What will really happen when these brand new organisms are growing in the fields, where they share the environment with millions of other plants? Scientists know that plant genes actually hop between species, because plant pollen (which fertilizes other plants) is carried on the wind, and the wind blows where it wills.

Christian farmers, environment activists, and many others—including the European Community, which has banned, severely restricted, or required the labeling of GMOs—are quite concerned about the release of genetically modified organisms (GMOs) into the environment. They are also concerned about the industry campaign, backed by the U.S. and Canadian governments, to stop GMOs from being labeled as such.

I will deal with the environment issue in my next column. For now, let us look at the labeling issue. It sounds a little dramatic to put it this way, but the Canadian government literally doesn't want you to know what you are eating.

U.S.-based Monsanto has put billions of dollars into GMOs, and they are determined to recoup their investment. One of their most important concerns is that GMO products should not be labeled, because customers may avoid them. The American government, like the Canadian government, seems anxious to help the companies. For example, U.S. Senator Bond told Thailand recently that the environmental concerns are "hogwash" and that labeling is unnecessary. (Thailand decided to label them anyway.)

The industry claims that the products don't need to be labeled because there is no danger. (In other words, Monsanto doesn't think you have the right to information that would enable you to decide for yourself.) People with allergies and those with celiac disease are worried because gene splicing may trigger reactions from foods that they would have considered safe. They need labeling to protect themselves. All the help they are getting from the Canadian government is the pronouncement that labeling is useless because GMO plants are mixed up with others anyway. If that is true, then either 1) the experiment should stop immediately or 2) the GMO plants should be segregated.

Already, GMO plants have made their way into Canada, in

the form of a type of canola engineered to withstand a heavy dose of pesticide. According to the Mennonite Central Committee, farmers they surveyed now use two to five times as much pesticide on their canola (margarine base). Hope you like pesticide with your margarine.

Christian environment groups, as well as others, want the GMO plants labeled. In November, 1999 the Christian Farmers Federation of Ontario called for mandatory labelling of genetically engineered food. They have conducted a number of think-tanks on the issue in recent years and their message, while complex in details, is simple in character: fundamentally, we want the consumer to be able to trust us. This requires labeling. Recently, the Mennonite Central Committee also put out some study papers, authored by Ian Ritchie, which I recommend, examining these issues (contact iritchie@escape.ca).

Ritchie says human beings certainly have the right to manage nature for the benefit of both ourselves and the created order, as in Genesis. The question is not whether we should use technology, but what is a wise use of technology? He comments, "Scientists still speak of there being an implicit rightness or order in all things. Evidence of this is seen in the fact that fish, for example, cannot mate with tomatoes, and fruit flies cannot mate with polar bears. Biologists point out that even if one allows for millions of years of evolution these diverse species still could not mate." So the big biotech companies want to release into the environment and then market to us creatures that could never exist in nature at all. And, they will assure us that there is so little danger that we do not even need to be able to find out what we are eating.

Ritchie also notes: "Martin Luther said that the creatures are 'the mask of God,' that they reveal something of God's face to us. What does it say about our trust in God's creative wisdom when we decide that we have a better idea about how to engineer nature?"

18 Does Our Environment Need Another Threat?

Christians should not trust that the "unseen hand" of the free market will somehow make everything come out right. Its function is only to react, and that is not enough where environment issues are concerned.

To those who think there is no danger from simply introducing genetically modified organisms into the environment via agriculture, I would address a simple question: How many more brand new challenges do you think the environment can take?

Most recent environment disasters which result in losses of stability, diversity, health, and livelihoods, are the outcome of the exact scenario that is happening with GMOs. The scenario goes something like this:

1) A company has invested big money in a technology and needs to recoup the investment. The technology will probably do environment damage but the company can risk that, because it will not be financially or otherwise liable for most of it. It hires a good public relations firm.

2) The profits from the technology create jobs and a tax base. Unions, trade organizations, and government discover the environment damage, but they are all badly compromised. They do not want to endanger jobs or tax revenues.

3) By now all parties, except for a few environment activists, have a strong interest in covering up the problem. Even when the problem becomes a crisis, the stakeholders make only half-hearted efforts to deal with it.

Our Atlantic and Pacific fisheries have collapsed due to this increasingly common scenario. Will agriculture be next?

Actually, there are warning signs already. Slip-ups have

occurred. For example, seriously contaminated genetically modified canola seeds produced by Monsanto Canada were released for sale (*Globe and Mail*, January 4, 2000), in an incident that, according to the Canadian Food Inspection Agency, sent "shock waves" through the industry. The industry, of course, pointed out that the incident did not become a disaster. Fine, but remember that in nature, the major safeguard is a very basic one— fish do not mate with tomatoes. Why should we settle for a lesser standard that includes these incidents?

Small-scale farmers from around the world met in Montreal in January to ask for a Biosafety Protocol, that is, regulations to protect the environment from the accidental spread of engineered genes. Canadian farmer Hart Haiden told Associated Press that genes from genetically engineered canola plants have already spread to unaltered varieties. He, and other farmers there, worry that, because European countries may ban imports of GMO canola, even farmers who do not use it may get shut out of a major market. Similarly, organic farmers, who must follow very stringent regulations in order to be certified organic, told the UN-sponsored meeting that they are particularly concerned because honeybees can carry pollen from canola for up to five miles (8 km). (Associated Press, January 26, 2000) So far, the United States has succeeded in preventing any plans for protection from getting off the ground, because of the heavy capital investment in this area. (See the numbered scenario above.)

As a journalist, I note how gleefully the biotech industry press jumps on any study that shows that during a particular season in a particular area no superweed developed. In reality, the whole enterprise is an accident waiting to happen.

The industry's explanation for this experiment with the planet's gene pool is unconvincing. It claims that GMOs are necessary to feed the Third World. Well then, some of us would be interested to know why Monsanto is buying a company involved in research on the Terminator Gene (Delta & Pine Lands). Terminator, which prevents a crop from producing fertile seed, is widely denounced by the world's agricultural scientists as a disaster for traditional Third World communities that have little cash and save seed from year to year. At present, no doubt due to the agriculturists' outcry, Monsanto has backed off on the plan.

Is there any role for gene transfer in agriculture? Probably there is. As Christians we should not oppose technology. We are stewards of God's creation, so we must determine wise uses. But nonetheless our viewpoint should be fundamentally different from that of the American biotech industry: As the Mennonite Central Committee points out in a recent study paper, Christians should not trust that the "unseen hand" of the free market will somehow make everything come out right. The free market does not predict and take steps to prevent disaster, as a wise steward should. Its function is only to react, and that is not enough where environment issues are concerned.

The "unseen hand" did not save the fisheries and it won't save agriculture. Strict environment and land use planning might, though.

19   Christian Farmers Decry "Suicide Gene" in Seeds

Biotech firms are trying to breed a gene into the seeds they sell that kills the second generation. That would force every farmer to return to the seed company and buy every year.

The Christian Farmers Federation of Ontario (CFFO) has expressed alarm over a new development in biotechnology that may threaten farmers around the world: the "terminator gene."

Farmers save purebred seeds from wheat, rice, soybean and cotton crops and plant them again. Bags of good seed have been sold, stolen and traded from time immemorial. But the future of the seed itself has been considered common property. Not any more.

Biotech firms, anxious to prevent farmers from simply saving successful seeds and planting them again, are trying to breed a gene into the seeds they sell that kills the second generation. That would force every farmer to return to the seed company and buy every year.

"It's turning lots of people who were good entrepreneurs, good managers of the creation, into pawns of large corporations," said Elbert van Donkersgoed, research director for the Guelph, Ontario-based farmers group.

One sore point is that the biotech company would never really sell the terminator seed to the farmer, as in the past—only the right to use the company-franchised, non-reproducible product.

The issue arose in March 1998 when Delta and Pine Land Company, which controls 73 percent of the market in cotton seeds, was awarded a United States patent to engineer crops to kill their own seeds by generating toxins. The company, undergoing acquisition by biotech giant Monsanto of St. Louis, Missouri, shares the patent with the United States Department of Agriculture. The toxin scheme is only one of several applications that the patent for "Control of Plant Gene Expression" covers.

CFFO is not the only group to oppose this scheme. The Consultative Group on International Agricultural Research, the world's largest agricultural research network, slammed the development in October 1998. It described the plants' "suicidal tendencies" as a nightmare for the developing world's farmers. Group researchers vowed instead to concentrate on high-yield, disease-resistant varieties whose seeds can be used again, to provide what they say is an urgently needed boost in world food production.

CFFO is right to be concerned, says Jeremy Rifkin, a long-time watchdog of the biotechnology industry and director of the Foundation for Economic Trends in Washington, D.C. Most of the world's seed companies have already been bought up by a few biotech corporations that have patented seeds, he told *Faith Today*. He describes the farmer's future relationship to the seed companies as the "new serfdom." "Farmers will be at the complete mercy of a handful of life science companies," he insists.

Other concerns have also been raised about terminator genes: 1) they may spread to neighboring fields of non-terminator plants of the same species and, through cross-pollination, kill their seeds as well; 2) soil, fungi and animals maybe harmed by the terminator's toxins, upsetting a regional ecological balance; 3) unwanted toxins could end up in food if terminators spread from a non-edible to an edible crop of the same species; and 4) because not all genes are activated in the first generation, terminators can escape into the general plant species gene pool, causing unexpected environmental problems later.

There have already been accidents with genetically engineered crops: hybrid oilseed crops, engineered to resist weed-killing chemicals, unexpectedly produced "superweed" offspring that have no food value but are equally immune to weed killers, according to 1997 reports.

North American corn and other descendants of native species that are related to roadside weeds are especially likely to cause problems. Engineered "super" corn or other such crops may pollinate their weedy relatives that may be growing in a nearby ditch to produce superweeds, 1998 research suggests.

Both van Donkersgoed and Rifkin stress that they are not opposed to biotechnology as such, but rather to developments that produce public losses for the sake of private gain. In fact, most CFFO members express cautious optimism about biotechnology in a recent membership survey, but they reserved condemnation for the terminator gene.

Despite their overall optimism, the 4,100 CFFO members are divided on many other biotechnological issues such as bovine growth hormone additives, van Donkersgoed said. So far, Canada has refused to allow the hormones, which also are promoted by the Monsanto Corporation, but some CFFO members want to use them.

Rifkin thinks that concerned groups such as CFFO need to develop more consensus on such issues and communicate it to the public, rather than reacting only when they sense immediate harm to themselves. "If each individual constituency, maybe women or farmers or environmentalists, speaks up only when they're hurt, it's going to be very difficult to challenge," he warns. "Whoever controls those genes controls the geopolitics of this coming century" since they will effectively control the world food supply.

Although the terminator technique is now understood, it will not be available until perhaps 2004.

20 Unholy Harvest? Evangelicals Join Protests of Genetically Modified "Frankenfoods."

Some Christian agriculturists question the right of American biotech companies to patent and own life forms such as seeds.

As bioetchnology moves from the petri dish to the produce aisle, Christian environmentalists are asking this difficult question: do genetically modified (GMO) crops, or so-called frankenfoods, violate Christians' biblical mandate to care for the Creation?

For many environmentally minded Christians, the issue is both a matter of social justice and environmental care. GMO crops may be the key to feeding burgeoning world populations, but detractors fear such crops will make the world's poor dependent on a few multinational biotech corporations. Also, the effect of these foods on consumer health and the environment is largely unknown. Mainline Protestants have been more outspoken on GMO concerns, says Ann Alexander, chairwoman of the Christian Environmental Council. But the issue will make the agenda at the Christian Environmental Council (largely evangelical in orientation), which meets in October 2001 in Milwaukee.

ENDING WORLD HUNGER?

GMO crops have genes cut and spliced from various plant or animal sources that would not mingle in nature. Biotech companies can breed plants that have high nutrient levels, or tolerate huge doses of herbicide. But detractors say that these modified plants may mutate in the environment, producing "superweeds" and making poor countries' problems worse.

The most controversial modification is Mississippi-based Delta and Pine Lands' work on a "terminator gene." The gene, under development, would prevent farmers from saving cotton seed by creating a toxin that renders its seed infertile, killing the next generation of the crop. Many agricultural communities around the world depend on saving seed from year to year.

Yet GMO foods may curb starvation and increase nutrition in Third World countries. "Technological advances generated, in the last few decades, enough food to feed one half-billion mouths that would have been unfed otherwise," says Michael Barkey of the Acton Institute for the Study of Religion and Liberty, an advocate of free enterprise and private property rights. He cites the example of Vitamin A rice, which may help prevent blindness.

BEARING FRUIT

Some Christian agriculturists question the right of American biotech companies to patent and own life forms such as seeds. "I find this to be morally repugnant, because if there is one thing in the Creation that should be free, it is the ability to enable fruitfulness on the part of seed-bearing plants," says Delmar Vander Zee, professor of biology and environmental studies at Dordt College in Iowa.

The United States is the world leader in promoting GMOs. Transgenic plants have been grown commercially in the U.S. since 1995. More than 70 million acres were planted in 1999, including vegetables, fruits, and cereal grains, much of it intended for export to Europe.

Nonetheless, American evangelicals have been slow to consider the issue—in part, says Peter Bakken of the Au Sable Institute (an environmental study program serving many Christian colleges), because many evangelicals endorse free-market economics and do not see agricultural technology itself as problematic.

REVENGE OF THE SUPERWEED

Playing God with the creation of food may have dangerous ramifications for the environment. But from the official world of science, the signals are mixed.

The American Academy of Sciences came down neatly in the middle on GMO crops in April, 2001, saying no evidence shows they are unsafe, but also recommending more study and regulation.

"What they're saying is they haven't released any evidence" on harmful effects, Vander Zee says. The spread of genes to wild relatives of crop plants—creating superweeds—has been documented in the United States. Potentially harmful GMO seeds were sold in Canada earlier this year, sending shock waves through the industry.

Barkey, however, insists that the terminator technology solves the superweeds problem by ensuring the seeds die before they can mingle and mutate with other seeds.

"We have all kinds of history of big corporations running the experiment at the public's and the Creation's expense, later to find out you can't back up," Vander Zee charges. "That doesn't prove this to be dangerous. What it proves is that we tend to want to move ahead faster than we know is safe."

Christian farmers often feel caught in the middle. They fear that Europe, which does not want GMO foods, is creating a trade barrier against American imports. "GMO differentiates American crops from European," says Dennis Schlagel, executive director of the Fellowship of Christian Farmers International. "So it's a great political strategy to segment American GMO crops out of Europe."

But Europe's move actually was consumer-driven, says Winnipeg-based ethicist Ian Ritchie. European consumers, burned by incidents like Mad Cow Disease, are much more skeptical than Americans about claims that a high-tech food is safe and environmentally friendly. All sides are bracing themselves for a recently announced advertising blitz from biotech companies, which hope to recoup their research costs by convincing consumers that GMOs are harmless.

Christian environmental activists want to look beyond the hype to identify responsible positions consistent with the Evangelical Declaration on the Care of Creation, Alexander says. Scott Althouse of the Evangelical Environmental Network suggests that they begin by asking: "How does it affect humanity and Creation's ability to praise God?"

21 Lessons From Walkerton: But Is Anyone Listening?

If government can't even ensure clean water in Ontario, how will it deal with largely unknown biotech risks?

Today, the independent judicial inquiry starts in Walkerton, Ontario, where last May thousands of people were poisoned by the runoff from cattle manure in their drinking water, and seven died. With luck, this will be a wake-up call to Canadians about the real state of our water supply—but don't count on it.

Most strains of E. coli live harmlessly in the intestines of humans and animals. But some strains produce powerful toxins; hence the need to keep bacteria out of drinking water. Yet, for over twenty years following 1978, when a dangerous well was first tapped in Walkerton, tests showed that the water supply was often contaminated.

But the warnings written in the water were cast to the winds. Unbelievably, according to the *Toronto Star* (October 14, 2000), on over fifty separate occasions, one or another authority could have taken action and every one failed. The public was never told.

Then, on May 17, 2000, after a severe rainstorm, over two thousand people became ill with one of the deadliest forms of E coli (O157:H7). Most recovered, but some children and old people began to develop a bloody diarrhea. Of these, seven died.

If you want to blame Premier Mike Harris and the cold-blooded Tories for cutting costs, go ahead. But during the two decades when two Walkerton wells were frequently pumping poisoned water, every major political party in Ontario held office. This is the main reason you are not hearing as much grandstanding from the opposition benches as you might expect. If they are much better than the Tories, they can't use their record in office to prove it.

The evidence clearly shows that ignoring water quality issues was a normal procedure across the province for decades. Essentially, water creates a simple political problem: water conduits are out of sight, which means that, to operate in an environmentally sound fashion, the politician must raise water rates in order to spend money on something the public can't see. Most politicians prefer to build the highly visible Councillor Jones Library or Reeve Smith Community Centre instead. And they can trust the public for one thing: it will never ask why water rates are not going up.

Many communities across Canada are no more cautious than Walkerton, according to reports. They are just lucky that Walkerton happened first.

Some people believe that the judicial inquiry will point us towards solutions. But judicial inquiries come and go. A number of destructive national myths keep us from building and paying for environmentally responsible water services. You can find one of these myths right on Walkerton's Web site (http:// town.walkerton.on.ca). The town is described as "on the shores of the beautiful Saugeen River," with "unmatched canoeing and fishing territories."

Yes, this is the greatest myth of Canada—a pristine, inexhaustible supply of pure, life-giving water. It is true that Ontario is one of the world's largest reservoirs of fresh water, but we pollute it without conscience, and then just cover up the warnings. That Walkerton should have happened in, of all places, Ontario is inexcusable, but does anyone even notice the irony? Another irony: right above the Walkerton blurb for water activities is a banner, "Relief fund donations can be made to any Town of Walkerton Bank" Imagine relief in Ontario for the cause of clean water!

There is also the myth of nature. Loren Wilkinson, a professor at Regent College who studies environment issues, points out that no one considers themselves responsible for a "free service of nature" like water. So national governments and multinational industries trade blame and consumers just vote to keep rates low. Disaster is inevitable.

Lastly, there is the myth of trustworthy government. Amazingly, for example, people are prepared to trust the government about biotechnology, saying, "Surely, we don't need labeling for biotech products because government scientists would tell us if it wasn't environmentally safe." Well, if "government scientists" can't even ensure clean water in Ontario, how will they deal with largely unknown risks?

The reality is that we have less reason than ever to trust governments than we used to. At one time, governments at least paid lip service to traditional religious values, under which deceit is wrong in principle. The politician might then have the grace to feel guilty. But a secular government does not need to believe that deceit is wrong, even in principle. Deceit enables both government and industry to function more efficiently. The costs can always be passed on to those who don't know or can't protest.

As Christians, our first priority should be to insist on honest disclosure from anyone whom we would reward with our vote.

22 Superbugs: Nature Fights Back Against an Over-Medicated Society

Recently, Swedish researchers discovered that salmonella bacteria were taking only 18 to 36 generations to mutate into dangerous forms, resistant to most antibiotics. That's a pretty quick trip down the family tree because bacteria can reproduce every twenty minutes.

Do you think you should go on antibiotics every time you come down with an infection? If so, you may not know it, but you are contributing to the growth of "superbugs"—bacteria that are resistant to antibiotics.

We're all familiar with the "miracle" story of antibiotics. These poisons, originally developed by molds and bacteria for the purpose of killing other molds and bacteria, have been taken by missionary doctors to every corner of the globe. Local, unresistant bacteria just drop dead in their wake, leaving people cured who would certainly have been goners otherwise.

That story is true. But another story is growing up in its wake that is more unsettling: the growth of "superbugs." These tough-nut bacteria eat antibiotics for breakfast. And the scientists who develop new antibiotics are having a hard time keeping up with them.

Bacteria are simple one-celled creatures that lack a cell nucleus. Their numbers were recently estimated. The sum is too large to express conveniently except in scientific notation. Scientists say that there are 5E + 30 bacteria, which means 5 with 30 zeros following—that looks a little odd but it is much easier than writing out all the zeros.

Bacteria are the most adaptive of living creatures, with an amazing variety of strategies for survival. Most live under the soil and helpfully make dead things disintegrate. This frees up the otherwise wasted nutrients for new, living things. A few bacteria make wine, cheese, or other pleasant or useful products. Some live in the digestive tracts of grass-eating animals and enable them to digest food. But a very few cause serious human or animal diseases by overwhelming our immune systems with their sheer, toxic numbers.

Recently, Swedish researchers discovered that salmonella bacteria were taking only 18 to 36 generations to mutate into dangerous forms, resistant to most antibiotics. That's a pretty quick trip down the family tree because bacteria can reproduce every twenty minutes.

It was also reported at a recent news briefing sponsored by the U.S. National Foundation for Infectious Diseases that strains of bacteria have begun to pop up that are resistant to the current "last-defense" antibiotics, methicillin and vancomycin. Years are expected to pass before newer equivalents are developed. A predicted increase in superbugs in the meantime may leave people with serious diseases in a vulnerable condition.

Why do bacteria become resistant to antibiotics? Because, due to their sheer numbers, cited above, there are bound to be a few that survive an assault. Since the scant survivors are the only ones that reproduce (which bacteria constantly do simply by dividing into equal halves), they pass on to their millions of one-celled offspring the capacity to laugh at that antibiotic. After that, cutting back on the use of the antibiotic is of little help. Resistant bacteria don't care whether we use lots of it or only a little. The trick is to prevent resistant strains from developing in the first place by not introducing so many bacteria to new antibiotics.

Some scientists believe that new technologies will be developed soon that can fight the superbugs more effectively by shutting off their ability to produce toxins (poisons). They think that the bacteria will never develop a resistance to the procedure because bacteria only learn from huge catastrophes and the procedure doesn't kill any of them. But, even if that idea eventually works, disease specialists think we need to become more prudent with antibiotics in the meantime.

Recently, the magazine of the College of Family Practitioners in Canada featured articles on reducing the avoidable use of antibiotics, as a way of protecting their effectiveness in cases of true need. One way that we can all help is by not demanding antibiotics from our overworked GPs whenever we feel a little under the weather. We may be protecting people who need them more.

23 Things the Environment Movement Can Do to Win More Support From Christians

Today, if you prefer creatures that are free to be themselves, you are an environmentalist whether you accept the label or not.

In *The Biotech Century* Jeremy Rifkin argues that an appropriate response to biotechnology is to weigh the true benefits, accept what is good, and throw out the rest. The trouble is, many of our fellow citizens will think that developments that make us cringe are great advances.

How about this: Dogs who can't disobey you (they have partly robotic brains). Cats who can't disdain you (they have "master-pleasing" dog genes inserted). Can't you just picture the public relations blitz that will accompany these "advances"? The celebrity promotions? The ethical justifications?

Okay, so you personally would rather have creatures that are free to be themselves (messy, contrary, possibly dangerous, but not dumbed-down for a commercial market)? Then, whether you accept the label or not, you are an environmentalist.

The only major competitor to the biotechnology movement (we will improve nature by remaking it to our specifications) is the environment movement (we will renew the health of the planet by reversing the damage done by industrialism).

I am attracted in principle to the environment movement, but unfortunately, they lose me as soon as they introduce their buddies. I am not alone in this. Many people of faith are deeply suspicious for the same reasons as I am. Here are some problems environmentalists must address if they want to increase their influence among Christians:

1) *A tendency to rely on big government to force an environmentalist agenda on the public.* By and large, environment activists follow the socialist practice of relying on lobbying big government. They do not take the time to convince the grassroots public. As a result, populist movements like the Canadian Alliance become a home for anti-environment forces. And whenever a conservative government comes to power, it throws out or weakens environment legislation. Instead of bemoaning conservatism, I believe environmentalists should examine their own strategies. If they spent more time communicating with citizens, populist movements would become pro-environment. The Walkerton water crisis would be a good place to begin a discussion with ordinary townsfolk.

2) *A disastrous alliance with the population control movement.* In the early 1970s, environment activists started to associate their cause with population control. This was an interesting alliance because the population control movement, which started in the early 19th century, originally had nothing to do with environment. Clergyman Thomas Malthus (1766-1834) kicked it off, proclaiming that people increase much faster than the food supply, so

starvation is inevitable unless strict controls are imposed on the poor. Malthus was wrong but very influential. The idea of controlling the size of poor families was then picked up by Social Darwinists in the late 19th century. These people believed that Darwin's theory of evolution explained human society: the poor were simply unfit competitors in a struggle for survival, so limiting their numbers was an act of mercy. After World War II, Social Darwinism has led a somewhat shadowy existence. But the environment movement unwittingly revived it by providing a brand new justification for efforts to limit the poor around the world for the sake of the environment. Never mind that the rich, on average, use up a lot more environment than the poor. Population control movements always focus on the poor—it is their very nature.

Obviously, one planet cannot support an unlimited number of human beings. But education for women and rising standards of living cause birth rates to fall. By contrast, foreign-imposed population targets arouse legitimate suspicion among poor people about the true motives for concern. If the environment movement wants to gain the trust of the world's poor people, it should divorce the population control movement and focus on the need for sustainable development, to enable the world's children to have a future.

3) *Keeping foolish religious company.* Some environmentalists, convinced that the Book of Genesis gives a right to destroy creation (its real message is the exact opposite), welcomed people who want to revive the pr-Christian goddesses of Europe. Again, a little history is in order: The pagan religions of Europe finally died out in the 18th century—they are lamented in one of Wordsworth's sonnets:

> "The world is too much with us; late and soon,
> Getting and spending, we lay waste our powers:
> Little we see in Nature that is ours...
> ...Great God! I'd rather be
> A Pagan suckled in a creed outworn..."

Wordsworth was not a pagan and he knew he could not go back in time and become one. However, in the mid-19th century, some people who were turned off by the Industrial Revolution made up a "pagan" religion that suited them. As a Canadian philosopher pointed out a few years ago, the trouble with these pagan "goddess" religions is that their advocates don't really believe them. That's not very surprising under the circumstances. My advice to the environmental movement: if you need a religion, stick to Judaeo-Christian religion. The majority of the public claims to believe it.

4) *Apocalypses that don't happen.* Nowadays, the apocalyptic prophet of doom is more likely to be an environmentalist than a Christian sectarian. Both types have an embarrassing tendency to dabble with numbers taken out of context. The effect is the same: loss of credibility for true issues. Environmentalists can learn from the long and ludicrous history of failed religious prophecies of doom.

THREE

A Theory So True That Even Falsehoods Support It?

Recently, a friend who is an Ontario high school science teacher received an e-mail from a journalist who wanted to know if the teaching of the theory of evolution had become controversial yet in the province.

It won't be the journalist's fault if it hasn't. Following on the heels of the Kansas evolution controversy, some Canadian journalists have turned their attention to what is happening here in Canada. And they are concerned about the fact that in Ontario evolution is taught only in one Grade 12 biology course. There are scientific thinkers in the United States who would like to make evolution theory the basis of the teaching of all biology. So the idea is being floated that the Canadian science teachers are somehow "avoiding the issue."

My teacher friend's view, which seems to be a consensus among Ontario science teachers, is that it would be very difficult to teach a complex theory such as evolution *as a scientific subject* until the students had amassed what she calls "a fairly detailed background in general biology."

Ontario parents have expressed little dissent on the subject of evolution because most parents who want changes in education are concerned about assessment, discipline, and the need for rigorous course content. By rigorous course content they mean that the student should emerge with "a fairly detailed background in general biology." When evolution theory is best taught in that context is precisely the sort of thing we pay teachers to know.

But my friend was talking only about what the theory of evolution means in biology. The journalist had other concerns: "Many people argue that the theory of evolution has significance even outside the sciences—in philosophy and religion, for example. Do you think students who graduate without having taken the new Grade 12 biology class in which evolution is to be taught, and who therefore don't have a comprehensive view of the theory, will be at a disadvantage (in university? in general?)."

My friend replied that 1) what disciplines such as philosophy and religion teach is their own business, 2) high school is not the place to acquire a comprehensive view of anything, and 3) "biologists have a clear, precise, and limited idea of what constitutes evolutionary theory, including the evidence for it, the type of observation it purports to explain, and the type of prediction it makes."

She is right, of course, but I fear she may be shouted down. Over the years, many people have had far broader ambitions for the theory of evolution than hers. They purport to explain the rise and fall of human nations, religions, and civilizations, and even why men or women behave as they do. Interestingly, one reaction to this has been a worldwide resurgence in the growth of creationism, the belief that the world sprang full-grown from the hand of the Father. Michelangelo's "Creation of Adam" is surely the best artistic rendering of that idea in its simplest form.

The following columns deal with a variety of "origins of life" issues from whether the Big Bang really happened to the implications of finding life on Mars. All these issues have profound philosophical as well as intriguing scientific facets. For example, scientists who discount the Big Bang origin of the universe may have at least some religious motives for their dissent. What would life on Mars suggest about the uniqueness of life on Earth? And, on the subject of evolution, an important question emerges in "Butterfly Tales": Can a theory be so true that even falsehoods can legitimately support it? Or do falsehoods always undermine truth?

24   Back to School? Get Set on the Net!

Warning to students: This column is about fascinating time sinks. Always do your DULL homework before getting into faith and science issues.

It will soon be time for the students among us, 7 to 75, to take the Long Walk back to school for still-higher education…

So let me introduce you to some Web sites that might be of interest to Christian students who are vitally interested in faith and science.

First, let me say that in my opinion the Internet is the most wonderful interactive tool ever invented. Those of you who are younger than 25 today, you don't know how good you have it!

Hey, when I was a child in the 1950s, I used to kick a can for something to do.

Everything you could find out about Mars was known. Everything you could find out about germs was known. Same went for plants, animals, the Earth, the Moon, Mercury, Saturn, and I don't know what else. It was Known and Written Down primarily because primitive tools made further knowledge impossible. But the people who wrote books did not put the problem quite that way…

In fact, all the books in the library said the same things, quoting from each other. That was called Knowledge. And the librarian locked it up with a key at five o'clock every single night.

Well, then came Sputnik (and Muttnik!), the electron microscope, the discovery of DNA, the Hubble Space Telescope, Voyager, environmentalism, and the Internet. Suddenly, the world become a place where New Things could be learned.

It is true, as some people are quick to tell you, that bad things have happened as a result of some of these discoveries. But weren't bad things happening in the world anyway?

Perhaps because my father was one of only a handful of survivors of an entire squadron of 250 men during World War II, I grew up with the idea that bad things do happen anyway. Good things happen when people make them happen.

Anyway, here are some fun good things that you might like to check out—three Web sites where you can get lots of good, free information on key faith and science issues for discussion or term papers:

Reasons To Believe is an international, interdenominational ministry established to communicate the way in which the discoveries of modern astronomy uphold belief in the Bible and support personal faith in Jesus Christ. Their Web site, http://www.reasons.org, provides a lot of clearly explained information about what those discoveries are and how they relate to religious beliefs (such as the idea that human life has meaning and that the universe has a specific origin). Note especially the Kids Space page with lots of great science links for kids.

Access Research Network is a non-profit organization dedicated to providing accessible information on science, technology and society that focuses on controversial topics such as genetic engineering, euthanasia, computer technology, environmental issues, creation/evolution, fetal tissue research, and AIDS. They provide some interesting information on science topics via their Web site at http://ww.arn.org

The reason for the warning that starts this page: When I was surfing these sites, I spent far more time on every one of them than I had intended and nearly missed my deadline.

Oh, and for Christian seniors especially—and seniors should always be learning—if you are interested in the relationship between faith and medical wellness, check into National Institute for Healthcare Research at www.nihr.org. There is lots of information out there on the relationship between a vital religious faith and continued good health in old age. None of us older types can afford to ignore that.

Hey, this academic year is going to be fun! I can just tell.

25   Did the Big Bang Really Happen?

Many people anchor their tent stakes very firmly in the sands of scientific orthodoxy. As long as the prevailing wind continues to blow big piles of sand over the stakes, everything is fine with them...

The "Big Bang" is the belief that the universe and every gravel pit, pond leech, thistle, and buggy software program in it started off as a cosmic explosion at zero time and zero space, perhaps twelve billion years ago.

As an idea, the Bang appeals to Christians, and to monotheists in general. We are told that in the beginning God created the heavens and the earth, out of nothing. Bang theory produces some very interesting footnotes to the text of creation. But we should realize that they are not the author's footnotes. They are merely a toiling editor's assessments.

Indeed, some dissent from the Big Bang has traditionally come from physicists with an orientation in Eastern religions. They find it easier to believe that the universe has always existed and perhaps that time endlessly repeats itself. Dissent was also urged on scientists who worked under communist rule because Bang theory has the politically inconvenient potential for suggesting that there could be a God out there somewhere.

Most recently, David Berlinski, a mathematician who enjoys making confetti out of overconfident science dogma, raised some interesting questions about the Big Bang in a recent edition of *Commentary*, a conservative intellectual Jewish magazine (February 1998).

The theory rests on the assumption that the universe is expanding, which means that, in general, the galaxies are moving away from each other and from us. But how do we know that the universe is expanding? In the late 1920s, American astronomer Edwin Hubble found that the light from distant galaxies was shifted to the red portion of the light spectrum, which is taken to mean that the galaxies are departing.

In that case, because the universe appears similar in every direction, its components must at one time have been closer together and therefore hotter. In fact, the theory assumes they were at zero distance from each other and their temperature was...well, of course, they exploded, and the shards are still travelling, and creating the universe you can see just a smidgen of if you get out of the city and look up on a clear night.

But Berlinski points out that Hubble was studying only 20 galaxies and that a more recent study of 10,000 has not confirmed the idea, suggesting rather that light patterns satisfy a quadratic law (the red shift varies with the square of brightness).

Berlinski is not claiming that he knows that the Big Bang did not happen. Rather, he says that too many findings that are inconsistent with the Bang are ignored because of the idea's high status as a governing secular myth. This is a common problem in the sciences today, he adds; bad news must come in battalions before it is heeded.

A year earlier, he touched off some really ballistic letters to the editor in the same magazine by pointing out the flaws in the commonly accepted reasoning of evolutionary biologists. It became quite apparent that many people anchor their tent stakes very firmly in the sands of scientific orthodoxy. As long as the prevailing wind continues to blow big piles of sand over the stakes, everything is fine with them...

What if, in the end, we cannot really confirm that the universe is expanding from a Big Bang? That will be a faith problem for people who must believe that they have zeroed in on Exactly How God Does Things.

I believe that Berlinski strikes the right note when he says of the creation of the universe in general, "The whole vast imposing structure organizes itself from absolutely nothing." Then he adds, "This is not simply difficult to grasp. It is incomprehensible."

Bang theory is one way of trying to comprehend creation. All methods of comprehension are doomed to fail in such a case. What people are really doing is having a lot of fun footnoting the text. Some footnotes are far more accurate and interesting than others, of course. Bang theory is one of the best. But, as Berlinski warns: "Beyond every act of understanding, there is an abyss."

At one point, the Lord asks Job, "Which is the way to the

home of light, and where does darkness dwell?" (Job 38:19) God
offers to explain everything to Job, provided Job can answer questions like that. But he can't, so God doesn't explain anything. And
we are free to continue puzzling over and footnoting the text.

26   God, Aristotle, and the Laws of Motion

*Does any human being grasp how big the universe is? The human
imagination does not operate as a calculator; it loses conceptual
power after applying the notion of "biggest."*

Father Jaki, a Hungarian-born priest, theologian, and physicist,
has an interesting perspective on the development of modern science. He argues that the classical world stumbled in its understanding of physics precisely because it believed in an eternal universe, rather than a universe with a beginning.

Today this idea, "creation from nothing within time" (*creatio
ex nihilo in tempore*), is familiar to us both from Christian theology
and the notion of the Big Bang. But Aristotle, the greatest thinker
among early Greek scientists, believed that such an idea was absurd. Jaki argues that, as a result of not believing in a first event,
the classical world could not formulate the first law of thermody-
namics (change of energy in a thermodynamic system equals heat
transferred minus work done) or the laws of motion generally.

It is not that they didn't try. They formulated all kinds of laws,
including laws that anybody could disprove. For example, one
suggested law was that a body that is twice as heavy as another
will fall twice as fast. (Try it. You won't need time on the Cray
supercomputer; you can use the back stairs.)

The notion of a beginning to the universe which, Jaki argues,
was fundamental to the first law, developed in its earliest form
among the Church Fathers and was made a dogma at the Fourth
Lateran Council held in 1215 A.D. In his monograph "Christ and
Science," he argues that not only monotheism but Christology
was essential for this understanding. Father Jaki, who won the

Templeton prize in 1987 for his contribution to the understanding between faith and science, has written almost forty books, many on the history and philosophy of science. Currently, he teaches at Seton Hall University in New Jersey.

Father Jaki also accepts the theory of evolution as the origin of life, as he explained in a talk he gave in Toronto on April 30, 2000. He believes that there is an irreconcilable opposition between Genesis 1 and modern science. But he does not so much discuss the account in Genesis as he dismisses it. He argues that the author of Genesis 1 (whom he believes to be Nehemiah) saw the universe only as a sort of big sky tent, and that he was not particularly interested in creation at all but was concerned only to make sure that people celebrated the Sabbath by demonstrating that even God celebrated it.

I have several difficulties with Father Jaki's viewpoint in this area: Nehemiah may well have thought the universe was a big tent. But does any human being grasp how big the universe is? The human imagination does not operate as a calculator; it loses conceptual power after applying the notion of "biggest." Mathematics can be done, but it cannot really be experienced. I don't think Nehemiah was worse off than we are in this respect.

As T.S. Eliot has pointed out, the sheer size of the universe is quite properly uninteresting to most human beings except as a statistic. After all, if a single bacterium were discovered on Mars, even if it was long dead, it would be far more interesting to most of us than the discovery of another hundred galaxies about which nothing new or different is known. And surely we are right. After all, the bacterium, however simple, or long dead, would have once been alive, and the implications are profound. But sheer distance, sheer size, or sheer longevity...what about it?

More generally, following C.S. Lewis, I am reluctant to position a historical figure like Nehemiah on one side of a controversy that did not arise in his lifetime. Nehemiah, for example, knew that the Lord "...created the heavens, the highest heavens with all their host/the earth and all that is on it..." (Neh 9:6a). He made no distinction between knowing who God is and what he does, and thinking that the people should follow the law they were given on Mount Sinai. The experience of rebuilding the temple from burnt rubble amid strong opposition undoubtedly sharpened his views; knowing more about far galaxies would not have changed them. Describing him as concerned only to get people to keep the Sabbath assumes that the question arose and then places him on one side of it (the narrow-minded one). But there is no clear reason for making that assumption.

So we are back with Genesis 1—easy to reconcile with scientific thinking in principle, but difficult or impossible in the particulars.

27   Key New Evidence in an Old Debate

The cells that make up our bodies are extremely complex. Before the development of the electron microscope, scientists assumed that cells would be simple little jellies that could somehow arise naturally from the six organic elements.

Hush. I think my editor has gone on vacation.

That means I can tackle a subject he told me not to touch. The temp proofreader won't interfere unless I misspell something...

The editor told me not to get into the creation-versus-evolution controversy. It generates almost as many heated letters as his editorials on the activities of maverick preachers. But, spurred on by the kind suggestion of reader Ron Bestvater of Weyburn, Saskatchewan, I got hold of and read Michael Behe's book, *Darwin's Black Box* (Free Press, 1996). This is worth taking a chance for. Students heading back to classes soon need a good reference source if this subject comes up.

Behe, a biochemist, seems to have fundamentally changed the nature of the argument by focusing not on animal or plant behavior but on biochemistry, that is, on the chemical processes within cells that make life possible.

The difference is critical because the cells that make up our bodies are extremely complex. Darwin did not know that. Before the development of the electron microscope, scientists assumed that cells would be simple little jellies that could somehow arise naturally from the six organic elements.

Most biochemistry has been done in the last half century. Its results do not filter back to the public very quickly, for reasons that become obvious when you try reading a biochemical explanation of how something like the eye or blood clotting works.

How does biochemistry affect the debate on creation vs. evolution? Well, consider the controversy over whether a complex eye can evolve over time from a simple photosensitive patch, such as a jellyfish might have. Behe does not argue about whether a complex eye can evolve from a simple one. Instead, he asks, how "simple" is this original patch anyway? What precisely happens when a cell becomes photosensitive? Behe is nothing if not precise. He quickly demonstrates that converting light into a signal within a nervous system is not simple at all.

Here's the nub of the problem: Behe calls cells "irreducibly complex." He means that there are no "simple" cell systems that could just arise by chance and then evolve into complex systems. That is because there is no simple way of doing the jobs these systems do and few if any possible variations. A creature with a simpler arrangement could not live at all. And there is little room for random variation. A little malfunction here or there and the cell does not evolve; it dies.

So, he asks, how could a system that must be very complex and completely successful the moment it comes into being arise by chance? In fact, his literature search shows that few people have even tried seriously to come up with a convincing explanation. None have succeeded.

Behe is not saying that evolution does not occur. He is saying that it may very well occur but it cannot account for the origin of life as we know it. Within the age of the present universe, chance does not produce the complex molecular machines that form the building blocks of life. You may just as well hope that a brand new car will "evolve" for you from the available elements in an abandoned strip mine.

Behe believes, based on his observations, that there is an Intelligent Designer behind the origin of life. He wisely avoids getting any more theological than that. Thus, rather than criticize his theology, readers must think carefully about what he is actually saying.

So significant are these new issues that some scientists actually believe that life may have been planted here by intelligent aliens. I know, I know. It seems like a foolish alternative to belief in God. It plays better in the movies though.

Readers who may discuss the creation-evolution controversy this fall with science teachers or students should definitely get this book. Those of us who have never taken courses in biochemistry may be tempted to skip the details and just feel guilty about neglecting them. But don't. Plough through at least some of Behe's explanations in order to grasp the fact that talk about "simple one-celled creatures evolving by chance" would have been a lot easier in Darwin's day when people had no idea what really goes on inside a cell.

28 Kansas School Board Decides to Dump Evolution

If there are no simple organisms, there should be no simple theories either.

A lot of newspaper ink has been sprayed around lately over the decision by the Kansas Board of Education last August to eliminate almost all mention of "evolution" from the state's assessment tests.

The new policy does not mean that teachers cannot teach, or indeed promote, the theory. It just means that it does not form part of the curriculum on which students are tested.

Most likely, an American court will soon mandate that the traditional evolutionary theory be reinstated as a test question.

Before the courts put a stop to further enquiry, however, some of the more frantic headlines in the American media deserve closer scrutiny. For example, we have been informed that evolution is "the most important concept to modern biology" by the National Academy of Sciences (*Chicago Tribune*, April 10, 1998).

The "most important concept"? Excuse me...

More important than the definition of living versus non-living things? More important than, say, the role of genes, of cell biology or photosynthesis (the way plants make food for themselves and animals)? More important than the life cycle of organisms (how they grow, reproduce, and die)? The water cycle? The breakdown of dead organisms by bacteria, with the result that other organisms can recycle them?

If "evolution," a theory about how organisms change over very long periods of time, a theory that has always been fraught with problems, has really become "the most important concept" in modern biology, then we do have a problem.

But the problem is not with the Kansas Board of Education. The problem is with the focus of teaching about the living world around us.

All of the items I mentioned above are immediately essential to the continuation of life on earth today. But if the theory of evolution were confuted by some discovery tomorrow, biological life would go on exactly the same, entirely as a result of the processes I have mentioned, and of others I forgot to mention, and of some I have never heard of and perhaps wouldn't understand, and of additional processes that no one has described yet.

None of these has anything to do with theories of evolution. They are entirely concerned with how life continues from one 24-hour day to the next.

In the real world, the theory of evolution is far down on the list of importance, in terms of explaining what happens. It may or may not describe what happened in the past and it certainly has no predictive power in explaining what will happen in the future. You can't say that about the water cycle or photosynthesis.

A high school biology teacher told me recently that the reason that evolution has suddenly appeared as the "most important principle" is simply because it is coming under attack, and many interest groups are rushing to defend it.

It is not surprising that the theory is coming under attack. There are a lot of problems with it. Here are a few: The simple examples that were supposed to prove Darwin's original views have never materialized. While small variations in life forms are common, changes that clearly produce new species are very hard to document.

Anyway, most genetic changes that make any difference are actually quite bad for the creature they happen to. Consider human genetic problems, for example. Even if a genetic change conferred a survival advantage 100 generations down the road, that would provide no assistance to the person today, when it matters.

The evolution theory also keeps changing to accommodate new findings that do not confirm Darwin's original views. Thus, some people use the word "evolution" to mean any observed variation in the present-day behaviour of a bacterium in the presence of an antibiotic, but then go on to apply it to conjectures about the origins of creatures (including human beings) where there are huge gaps in the record and many problems with the application.

But, for my money, biochemist Michael Behe's challenge is the most serious problem for the theory of evolution.

Darwin's theory assumed that what happens inside the individual cells that make up all of us is a simple, mechanistic process that could just, sort of, happen. Well, if you think that, dream on. The complexity of cells grows with each passing discovery. As Behe remarked in a recent interview, when we discussed bacteria, "there are no 'simple' organisms."

(Despite this, bacteria are presented to students as "simple" organisms.)

Well, if there are no simple organisms, there should be no simple theories either. But don't expect these issues to be examined by traditional science politics organizations any time soon. Too much is at stake.

29 Butterfly Tales: The Politics of Science Education

A theory that has every virtue except truth to nature is a theory in trouble.

Recently, according to the *New York Times* (August 13, 2000), the Kansas decision that the teaching of evolution should be optional was reversed. Apparently, this resulted from concern on the part of many parents that their children's educational future might be limited in a society where the science establishment is determined to teach the theory of evolution as fact.

Personally, I agree with Michael Behe that the theory should be taught, with the problems identified. But I sense that the Kansas parents know that their kids will get on better in life if they adhere to the party line and don't make a fuss.

The parents' hunch is undoubtedly true. But it doesn't make the party line true.

I have a number of reasons for thinking that the theory of evolution, as currently taught, is in trouble. But no reason seems so compelling to me as the fact that whether or not the theory is true has apparently ceased to matter. Let me give an example I came across quite recently: A mathematical series called Connected Models (available at www.ccl.sesp.northwestern.edu/cm) proposes to create modelling languages accessible to middle school students so that they can create models of large systems of interacting agents and objects.

One model the developer uses is the Viceroy—a common moth best known for looking almost exactly like the Monarch butterfly. (If you think you have never seen one, don't worry, you probably have, but you thought it was a smallish Monarch.) According to the theory of evolution, the Viceroy, a "Batesian (or Mullerian) mimic," evolved over a slow series of steps to look like the Monarch, because the Viceroy tastes good to predators, but the Monarch tastes bad.

Now there is one problem with this theory: researchers say

that the Viceroy does not taste good to predators. So looking like a Monarch confers no great advantage, at least not compared to the trouble of adopting almost exactly the same complex wing patterns as a member of an unrelated species.

So the state of the research is this: The Viceroy looks very much like the unrelated Monarch but nobody has any idea how it came to look that way. The evolutionary explanation is elegant and would be highly satisfactory, but apparently it isn't true. So for now, you would expect it to be discarded in favour of agnosticism on the subject.

But no such thing happens. Instead, the author of Connected Models writes, "Recent research now suggests that viceroys might also be unpalatable to bird predators, confusing this elegant explanation. Nonetheless, we have modeled the relationship anyway. Batesian mimicry occurs in enough other situations [snakes, for example] that the explanation's general truth is unquestionable. The monarch-viceroy story is so accessible and historically relevant that we believe it to be instructive even if its accuracy is now questioned." (The square brackets are in the original.)

Wow. This raises a lot of questions about what is going on in science education. If the story is true about snakes—as it may well be—why not write a model that concerns snakes? Why tell fairy tales about butterflies/moths and insist on the students treating them as fact when we know they probably aren't?

Above all, what does it mean to say that a story is "instructive even if its accuracy is now questioned"?

If we were talking about English Literature, I would know very well what that means, and it would be a valid point. For example, the tragic story told in *Romeo and Juliet* is a good example of material that is instructive even if it is not accurate to historical events. But no one attempts to ground a theory of Italian Renaissance history on the events portrayed in Shakespeare's play either.

But in science and math, if an inaccurate theory is instructive, it is only instructive when portrayed as an inaccurate theory. Otherwise, it is misleading.

If space permitted, I could supply other examples. But it seems quite clear that evolution is beginning to function in our culture in the same way that astrology did in the High Middle Ages. Today, it is conventional to ridicule astrology, but at one time it provided reasonable explanations, drawn from the movements of the planets, for otherwise baffling events.

After a while, the reasonableness took on a life of its own, even if the explanations were untrue. And that is exactly what is happening with evolution, which means that the suppression of dissent will not make the problems go away.

30 The Scopes "Monkey" Trial Revisited

If you enjoy faith and science issues, here's a book you should ask someone to buy you for Christmas: *Summer for the Gods: The Scopes Trial and America's Continuing Debate over Science and Religion* by Edward J. Larson (Basic Books, 1997).

In the summer of 1925, a small town in Tennessee became a hub of intense international interest when famed defence lawyer Clarence Darrow squared off against progressive politician William Jennings Bryan over a Tennessee law that forbade the teaching of the theory of evolution in schools. Although biology teacher Scopes, the defendant, was convicted of a misdemeanour, both sides considered the case a victory.

The really interesting part of *Summer for the Gods* (which won a Pulitzer Prize in 1998) is the difference between what actually happened and how the case was presented later, particularly in the stage play and movie, *Inherit the Wind*. Relying on massive documentary research, Larson cuts through layers of myth, and reveals much more interesting facts.

To start with, at the trial, almost nobody actually held the position that later commentators have claimed.

Most religious people of the day actually thought that evolution and the Bible could be reconciled. The issue was not controversial in the United States for many years. But some Fundamentalists, including Bryan, became concerned by the growth of Social Darwinism, a philosophy that conveniently justified social injustices as merely an outgrowth of Darwinian evolution—the strong killing off the weak. Bryan saw Darwin's theories as "the operation of the law of hate—the merciless law by which the strong crowd out and kill off the weak."

Bryan's charge sounds a little strong to modern ears. But he had reason to be concerned. Of six well-known scientists who would have testified in favour of evolution at the Scopes trial, none showed up, partly because they all favoured coercive eugenic measures (and Clarence Darrow opposed them). Biology textbooks reflected the scientists' view. In one edition, the text Scopes used (Hunter's *Civic Biology*) cheerfully announced, with regard to society's unfortunates, "If such people were lower animals, we would probably kill them off to prevent them from spreading." Obviously, the conflict between orthodox religious beliefs and this sort of belief goes much deeper than controversies about the Seven Days of Creation.

When, on Bryan's instigation, the Tennessee legislature banned evolution theories from the classroom, the legislators ignored his warning against setting a penalty. Thus they unintentionally set the stage for a possible martyr and a show trial.

The prosecution was not originally spearheaded by famed defence lawyer Clarence Darrow, but by the American Civil Liberties Union. ACLU, after losing out on various anti-patriotism efforts, was looking for an "individual liberty" platform and saw the Tennessee act as an opportunity. Darrow actually horned in on the ACLU case, because he saw it as a chance to attack religion. ACLU wanted to dump Darrow, precisely because they were trying to avoid a confrontation over religion. But Darrow stuck to the case like a fly and took it over from ACLU. Although he did humiliate Bryan on the witness stand, he probably alienated the jury.

And Scopes himself wasn't really a martyr. He was a well-liked football coach-cum-biology teacher who agreed at a meeting with friends at the local soda fountain to be the one who would be prosecuted. His way was paid to go to graduate school after the trial.

Incidentally, the town of Dayton, Tennessee, far from being the scene of massive intolerance, as it was later portrayed, revelled in the case, seeing it as a huge commercial opportunity and a chance to boost the "new South." Monkey dolls and paraphernalia turned up everywhere.

Nonetheless, the vast majority of townsfolk remained unconvinced by the theory of evolution. One reporter quoted a student's remark about Scopes that probably captured the attitude best: "I like him, but I don't believe that I came from a monkey."

Indeed, Larson offers a poignant observation: *Inherit the Wind* was written in the 1950s in reaction to McCarthyism. And, not too surprisingly, the "Bryan" character in the play has more in common with Joe McCarthy, who wrecked lives without apparent conscience, than with the Christian progressive politician of the 1920s who offered to pay Scopes's fine. By the 1950s, the gentility of the 1920s was not even a memory.

Fast forward: In 1982, when George Gallup Jr. asked the poll question, half of Americans said they did not believe in any theory of evolution, theistic or otherwise.

I suspect that groups like the ACLU, running to the courts to defend evolution, have done far more to discredit it than its opponents could. There is something odd in principle about a theory of science that always seems to need a legal defence fund.

And—this just in—following the recent Kansas decision, an Oklahoma state schoolbook committee has decided to put a disclaimer in textbooks stating that evolution is a controversial theory. Well, I guess few would argue with that.

31 New Magazine Helps Christians Understand Key Science Discoveries

The Bible does not focus on God as Creator. Yes, that is the starting point. But the text soon zeroes in on good and evil. And, despite occasionally taking up the theme of Creation again, the Bible remains focused on human lives and human choices.

Christians who are interested in the religious significance of the fantastic recent discoveries in deep space and in living cell biology should find a new quarterly glossy magazine, *Cosmic Pursuit*, a great read.

As I have mentioned in this space before, recent discoveries in biology have revealed a universe that is much more precisely and intricately designed than most scientists used to think. And this is also a universe where the smallest particles in physics do not even have to strictly obey what we once believed to be ironclad natural laws.

The significance of most of these finds has not yet filtered through our culture. Many people still think that the universe studied by space scientists is just an endless yawn of Nothing speckled by giant, floating rocks. But the concept of the "black hole" and the "quantum leap" have at least helped us understand that there are much stranger things in the universe than we once believed.

Scientists today are trying to come to grips with the implications of these new discoveries. *Cosmic Pursuit* was started by science journalist Fred Heeren to convey to the public the way in which all these discoveries point to an intelligent Creator. Heeren says that his own quest for the answers in these matters led him to faith.

Heeren interviews scientists engaged in cutting-edge pursuits, asking them what conclusions they have reached about whether the universe was created by an intelligent being. The results are very interesting. For instance, cosmic scientists have learned that the universe is very precisely organized. If it had departed even very slightly from exact specifications, it would not work.

George F. Smoot, who headed up the COBE satellite team that discovered the "seeds" from which galaxies grow, comments that "...when you start multiplying all the probabilities together, you find it's extremely unlikely that it's a random kind of chance, just like it's extremely unlikely that someone had my particular genes." (*CP,* Fall 1997)

Similarly, Robert Jastrow, director of NASA's Goddard Institute and of Mount Wilson's Observatories, comments that the discovery of a Big Bang—the origin of space and time at a precise point—is "a curiously theological result to come out of science." (*CP,* Spring 1998)

The magazine also reports on the discoveries in cell biology and genetics particularly the way in which the genetic code must be seen as an immensely complex "language." But the genetic code is not just any language, it is a language that can utter living beings. Who except God could invent such a language?

Now, none of this proves that the God we Christians worship exists or that any particular proposition in the Bible is true. The new discoveries do mean, however, that belief in God as the Creator of the universe is an entirely reasonable assumption, based on the evidence. More reasonable, in fact, than some of the alternative propositions that have been advanced.

One of these propositions is that alien life forms planted life here from another universe. Another is that new universes are constantly winking into and out of existence with each move we make. It seems to me that if a person cannot accept that there might be a Creator God, they would be better off just to say that they don't know how or why the universe came into existence than to believe such propositions as these.

But, exciting as these times are, we need to be careful to keep the proper biblical perspective in mind. The Bible does not focus on God as Creator. Yes, that is the starting point in Genesis 1:1. But the text soon moves on to zero in on the issues of good and evil in human lives. And, despite occasionally taking up the theme of Creation again, the Bible remains focused on human lives and human choices. From the Bible's point of view, that focus is entirely appropriate, because we are told that the universe we live in is doomed to pass away (Revelation 21:1) but that our final choices for good or evil are eternal (21:5-8).

At US$24.99, a subscription to *Cosmic Pursuit* would make a great gift for a science-minded young person or a school library. Reach them at The Day Star Network, 326 S. Wille Avenue, Wheeling, IL 60090, 1-800-743-7700 or www.daystarcom.org.

32 Worldwide Growth of Creationism Attracts Attention

Creationism said to be "mutating" and "spreading."

According to a Special Report in British-based science magazine *New Scientist* (April 2000), creationism is "mutating" and "spreading," and becoming a worldwide source of concern.

Considering the efforts of *New Scientist* and many similar publishers aimed at educated laypeople to debunk creationism, the two most likely explanations for creationism's survival and growth are 1) it is more persuasive than the Special Report suggests; and/or 2) debunking is a game any number can play, and players can start from any position.

Don't expect a discussion of either of these possibilities from *New Scientist*. But consider the cultural significance of what the publication's editors and authors do say.

The Special Report, available at www.newscientist.com, starts with the fact—apparently quite startling to the authors—that although the United States is a leading scientific nation, 47% of Americans and about 25% of American college graduates believe that human beings were specially created by God. Sixty percent said that students should be taught "both points of view" and should make up their own minds (according to a poll by People for the American Way, a liberal pressure group).

The really interesting claim that the report makes is that creationism, in the modern Western evangelical sense, is a growing belief worldwide, not a waning one. For example, creationism is now said to be taught at many state universities across Russia. I would guess that this is partly a reaction to previous state-enforced atheism.

Other examples are both inevitable and intriguing; for instance, in the last 27 years New Zealand creationists went from zero to 5% of the population. The chief converts are said to be Maoris and Pacific Islanders, whose experience of "scientific" European culture has hardly been liberating.

And in some countries, a few people have embarked on the futile process, pioneered by U.S. evolutionist groups, of using the courts to try to ban creationist ideas. The magazine recounts the case of Australian geologist Ian Plimer who sued a creationist for "trade fraud" in 1996. Plimer lost the case because the judge ruled that the creationists were not primarily engaged in trade. Unfortunately, Plimer was also bankrupted by his legal fees.

What to make of all this? There are more brands of creationism out there than soup, and some approaches make more sense than others, at least to me. But people listen to the creationist because their instinct about the universe is the same as his: they don't believe that the complex world we live in just happened by chance. The arguments about details (from the "days of creation" right down to story-stoppers like "where did Cain's wife come from?") tend to be discounted as quarrels among experts. I don't know what *New Scientist*'s editors imagine will change this situation— certainly not more debunking or U.S.-style litigation.

One book that *New Scientist* mentioned but did not address is biochemist Michael Behe's *Darwin's Black Box*. Behe, who is not committed to a creationist perspective, talks about the significance of the mind-numbing complexity of biochemistry for evolution theory. I suspect that Behe's challenge is the most significant one for the evolutionists because he asks some hard questions about "how, exactly" the complexity of the present order evolved when it is not clear that intermediary steps may even be possible. Presumably, it is easier for *New Scientist* to monger scare stories about the growth of creationism than to address questions such as his.

The report also contains an interesting comment by Bryan Appleyard, author of books on science issues. He takes evolutionists to task for attempting to pronounce on all kinds of subjects, often starting from very shaky foundations. He quotes traditional evolutionary "Just So stories" like the following: "Women don't kill their babies, because of evolution; but, on the other hand, if they do kill their babies, that must also be because of evolution." And he points out the obvious: "A theory that explains everything might just as well be discarded since it plainly has no real explanatory value." He also predicts more "science-bashing" as a likely outcome of the popularization of that kind of discourse.

No doubt Appleyard is right about the bashing. But surely, in cases such as the one he cites, the object of the bashing is not science as such but the shallowest brand of useless pop psychology, incorrectly labelled as some kind of science, and therefore properly bashed by anyone who needs to get some kind of a grip on the real issues of child abuse.

Several things have been lost in the debate, including the fact that many Christians are evolutionists, for example, Father Stanley Jaki, a Hungarian-born Benedictine priest and physicist. (See "God, Aristotle, and the Laws of Motion.")

33 Many Demonstrations of Evolution Turn Out to Be Myth

Remember what you learned about evolution in biology textbooks? Forget it!

With the publication of biologist Jonathan Wells's *Icons of Evolution* (Regnery Publishing, Washington, 2000), mainstream media are beginning to take the Intelligent Design movement seriously. Seriously enough, that is, to discuss its arguments, as opposed to merely denouncing them.

Icons of Evolution demonstrates that many pieces of evidence for evolution that you learned in biology class are actually discredited. Some have been discredited for a long time. Take Haeckel's drawings of embryos, for example. They show that embryos of vertebrate species are very similar, which suggest that they descended from a common ancestor. In fact, a theory even arose, and was taught to me in school in 1962, that human embryos pass through a fish, bird, and monkey stage, and only "become" human later.

This belief is one of the philosophical underpinnings of the legal abortion movement. It explains why your otherwise intelligent neighbours can seriously maintain that "the fetus is not a human being." Such a statement would make no rational sense to anybody except for the uses made of Haeckel's theories.

Haeckel's drawings were fakes. He altered the appearances of embryos to make them look more alike. He also left out those that did not fit his theory. More important, he assumed that in the early stages, embryos look most alike. In fact, they look quite different in the early stages, develop superficial similarities only in middle stages, and diverge again later. No true representation of embryos supports the textbook theories.

Wells talks about many other "icons of evolution": The peppered moth does *not* demonstrate evolution by turning dark in polluted environments. (The moths never consistently show that pattern.) The Darwin finch does *not* demonstrate evolution by altering its beak size. (Beak size waxes and wanes, depending on climate conditions.) Genetic experiments that produce four-winged flies do *not* demonstrate evolution in action. (To demonstrate evolution in action, the change must be random and beneficial—but four-winged flies cannot fly.)

The problem is *not* that these apparent demonstrations of evolution are mistaken. Anyone who advances a theory can be mistaken. Without theory, there is no way of organizing information.

The problem is that biologists knew for a century that Haeckel's drawings were fakes. No one said anything. The drawings and misstatements appear again and again in standard textbooks today. So do the other icons. When anyone complains that these are not truthful examples of evolution in action, they are accused of being a "creationist."

So why is perpetrating a fake more acceptable than admitting ignorance? Because, in some circles, evolution has become a religion to be defended against unbelievers. Truth is in real danger of extinction.

I believe that Christian parents should get and read Wells's book over the summer, ask teachers to read it, and then review the information that appears in their children's biology textbooks. We should *not* be trying to get schools to stop teaching about evolution, as some people have attempted to do. But we should insist that 1) discredited material has no place in our science textbooks and 2) the theory of evolution should be taught, warts and all. That is, data that does not support it must be presented along with data that does.

But maybe I am hoping for too much. Science may well be coming under the same sort of "postmodern" pressure as other disciplines. If people cease to believe that truth is content-based, that does not mean that they cease to believe in truth. Quite the contrary. They believe that truth is power-based. The most powerful group gets to posit their truth as the top truth. They get to identify non-supportive or contrary evidence as "dangerous nonsense" and use the resources of public institutions to mount an assault on it.

Of course, orthodoxies always behave this way, given a chance. But postmodernism makes one crucial difference: when the public believes in content-based truth, false orthodoxies are eventually forced to correct their errors or die. But when the public no longer believes in content-based truth, there is no external reason why a false orthodoxy must correct its errors. The option of stepping up the persecution against non-supporters can be pursued indefinitely.

If the textbook authors simply rush to defend their errors, they are making the theory of evolution into another "senseless idol,", about which its perpetrators never seem able to say "This thing I am holding is a sham." (Isaiah 44:20b) Still, fighting this stuff is definitely worth a try.

34   Little Green Men on a Little Red Planet

Science fiction amounts to a salvation scheme that substitutes technology for grace and clever ideas for sacrificial suffering.

Could there be life on Mars? Obviously, the Little Green Men have receded into the late, late movies. But the success of the Pathfinder expedition has renewed the serious debate.

Mars is thought to have the required elements for life. The trouble is, the red planet suffers from a truly lousy climate. The vicious pink dust storms are bad enough, but then there are those permanent arctic temperatures.

Still, some evidence suggests that Mars wasn't always as deeply depressing as it is now. The planet may even have been an early victim of global warming, followed by cooling. Hence the theory that simple one-celled creatures might live there.

Recently, creatures have been discovered here on earth that manage to live under dreadful conditions. These extremophiles have fueled the debate by challenging long-held notions about what a creature must have in order to survive.

For example, the Pompeii worm was found to thrive at 80 degrees Celsius (176 degrees Fahrenheit) around thermal vents in the ocean floor. Formerly scientists believed that 55 degrees Celsius (131 degrees Fahrenheit) was the upper limit for a complex creature's survival. And then there are "Hell's cells," colonies of bacteria that live thousands of metres beneath the earth's surface and can stand temperatures of up to 110 degrees Celsius.

None of this proves there is life on Mars, which is best noted for miserable cold rather than stifling heat. And in fact, when a potato-sized Martian meteorite (ALH84001) created an uproar last year because odd formations suggested that it once contained bacteria, it flunked the test. After an emotional debate, the consensus is that it does not contain any identifiable bacteria.

Skeptics suspect that some "life in space" sightings are exaggerated interpretations, aimed at boosting space exploration budgets in recessionary times.

But we can't rule out the possibility. After all, a million mete-orites can be lifeless and no one cares. But if even one shows extraterrestrial life, the Internet will crash more than a few times as people kill their trackballs for any information they can get about it.

The advent of small, light, low-cost robots that can go to Mars, transmit data, send back samples and then deteriorate without demanding compensation, means that we will soon be able to find out whether bacteria have ever lived there.

Suppose there was or is simple life on the red planet? Theo-logically, it shouldn't make any difference whether bacteria live on Mars, unless your theology requires you to believe that God could not allow bacteria to live there.

As C.S. Lewis pointed out long ago, the subject of extrater-restrial life only becomes theologically interesting if we find ra-tional, moral beings in another part of the universe and compare them to ourselves. That, of course, is the premise on which a hun-dred years of science fiction has been based.

But the chief difficulty with meeting any interesting space aliens off the movie set is that real intergalactic distances are in-comprehensibly vast. Right now, astronomers using the Keck II telescope are peeking at a galaxy (RD1) that is separated from us by over 12 billion light years.

So what if there is anybody that far yonder? The great globe, as Shakespeare put it, shall dissolve and this insubstantial pageant leave not a rack behind before we get to have a really good chat with them.

Science fiction usually tries to get around this difficulty by theorizing that the space aliens have figured out how to travel faster than light. In which case they should already be back on their own planet before they get here, shouldn't they? Einstein said it couldn't really happen.

More worrisome is the fact that science fiction also implies that the aliens' advanced technical skills or knowledge make them either superior to us or better able to fix our problems. In other words, the story really amounts to a salvation scheme that substitutes technology for grace and clever ideas for sacrificial suffering.

But after so many years of wishful thinking about flying saucers, we're still alone, and likely to stay that way. The only invasion we have experienced on earth is the one we celebrate at Christmas—though we are told to just as surely expect another one, date and time left blank.

FOUR

The Really Difficult Problems in Faith and Science

It seems to me that there are five really difficult problems that people of faith confront:

1) What does it profit a man if he gains the whole world and loses his own soul? (Jesus)
2) Am I my brother's keeper? (Cain)
3) If someone dies, will they live again? (Job)
4) Lord, why don't you just kill the wicked? (David)
5) Lord, why do the innocent suffer? (everybody)

Dealing with these five problems often causes people to despair and lose faith, as any pastoral visitor will attest. Most people, by contrast, do not care where Cain's wife came from. Let's get things in perspective here.

Interestingly, not one of the five problems listed above is likely to be affected by discoveries in science. That is because, as philosophers of science have often pointed out, science is not an enterprise that should even try to answer questions of this kind.

So when science dogma clashes with religious dogma, it should be at a minor intersection, not a major one. For example, people who discount miracles will not accept faith healing even when it happens. They will accept any other explanation, no matter how ludicrous. Similarly, people who believe that the Bible is full of secret codes will not accept the findings of information science, no matter how much light they shed.

But some people would like to make the scientific enterprise a sort of religion. It is most likely to be a religion based on "sociobiology." Sociobiology is a serious academic attempt to apply beliefs about the evolution of animals to transactions in human society. That or some other bogus religion might provide convenient answers to the difficult questions. For example:

1) What does it profit a man if he gains the whole world and loses his own soul? (He doesn't have a soul. So why worry?)

2) Am I my brother's keeper? (No. Only the strongest survive.)

3) If someone dies, will they live again? (No. So live for the present.)

4) Lord, why don't you just kill the wicked? (They're not wicked. Just misguided although, in reality, their methods work, so we're still working on exactly why they're misguided.)

5) Lord, why do the innocent suffer? (They're not "innocent." They're unfit. Only the strongest survive, remember?)

Obviously, if the sociobiologist is right, we are in big trouble. But if he is wrong, we are in a lot bigger trouble. Better assume he is wrong and go back to religious answers ("do justice and walk humbly with your God").

A more serious problem is that when science dogmas try to become orthodoxies for interpreting the world around us, they can involve us in distortions of fact. See, for example, "Butterfly Tales: The Politics of Science Education," where we are asked to blithely accept teaching to children a "fact" that is probably not true because it is more convenient than the truth.

In the same way, religious orthodoxies can also involve us in distortions when they demand proof that is not really available. For example, the Bible does not claim that it contains a secret code— indeed, a distinguishing feature of the Bible is its insistence that no special knowledge is required to find the way of the Lord, only a willingness to know it. So why insist on the existence of a secret Bible code?

Well, my columns are hardly the last word on the intersection between faith and science, but for those interested in some of these controversial topics, they might make a useful armchair tour.

35 Science: Stranger than Fairy Tales

If things keep going the way they are, the universe may become maddeningly difficult for anybody to understand—almost on a par with human nature.

Once upon a time, typically in the mid to late 19th century, a familiar sort of figure stomped the lecture circuit: the science lecturer who knew the Meaning of Things. The universe had been figured out, he said, and it operated according to the laws of physics and chemistry. And, of course, there was definitely no deity behind it...

If anybody had been fool enough to ask how we could be sure that the laws of physics and chemistry operate exactly the way the lecturer said they did, they would doubtless have been rewarded with a withering stare. The answer was simple: Experiment had proved it.

Fine. But people are always tinkering, so they experimented some more, just to be sure. And they soon discovered that the universe largely isn't the way the mid-19th century thinker supposed it was. In fact, in the 20th century, the universe has turned out to be so mysterious that it is actually very difficult for scientists to explain.

If things keep going the way they are, the universe may become maddeningly difficult for anybody to understand—almost on a par with human nature.

Consider, for example, the behaviour of quantum particles. These are the individual particles of energy or matter that are too small to be divided any further, such as individual photons of light. Quantum particles behave as if they are both individual bits and long waves at the same time. (No, it doesn't make sense. But bear with me.)

Quantum mechanics is the branch of physics that tries to study these particles. Albert Einstein, who discovered that time is relative, rather than absolute, rejected the findings of quantum mechanics because it suggests that space isn't absolute either. That outcome was too weird even for Einstein. Experiment, however, seems to back up quantum mechanics as well as it backs up Einstein's relativity theory, even though the two theories don't agree.

Many people use the expression "quantum leap" to mean a really big jump. For example, they will say, "Our office made a quantum leap in productivity when we got the new photocopier."

But a real quantum leap is a leap that is only possible if space does not exist, at least not in the sense that we usually suppose. That goes well beyond the efficiencies of a new photocopier.

For example, physicists have devised an experiment that forces a photon of light to act either on Path A or Path B. The photon acts on both of them, even though it would have to go faster than the speed of light (that is, faster than itself) to do so. Electrons—quantum particles charged with negative electricity—do much the same thing. When physicists try to sort a group of electrons by two different sets of qualities (for the sake of example, red vs. green plus long vs. short), the final assortment will alter itself to show only one distinguishing set of qualities. To accomplish this, the electrons have to know what's in the other box, and they apparently do. But how can they know if they're not there and can't get there?

Physicists explain the particles' strange ability to frustrate the sorting process by saying that they are nonlocal. That is, they don't have to be in only one place at one time. Science writer Timothy Ferris, puts it like this: "They act like an intimately connected whole, regardless of whether their parts are far removed from each other." (*The Whole Shebang*, 1997)

It is as if the astronomical increase in space that is supposed to have occurred since the Big Bang doesn't matter to the tiny particles. We should all be able to ignore distance, shouldn't we? But we larger beings seem to have lost the trick...

In fact, there may be lots of things in the universe that are weirder than the behaviour of quantum particles. But space, which exists for columnists if not for particles, forbids discussing them now.

We need to keep in mind the words of the writer of Ecclesiastes, "I have seen the task that God has given to mortals to keep them occupied. He has made everything to suit its time; moreover he has given mankind a sense of past and future, but no comprehension of God's work from beginning to end." And then he adds, "And he has done it all in such a way that everyone must feel awe in his presence." (Ecclesiastes 3:10-11, 14b, *Revised English Bible*)

36 Time Travel: Retro Revisited All Over Again

Relativity theory suggests that travel into the past might be possible if you can travel faster than light.

Is time travel really possible? Some people, of course, want to travel into a *Star Wars* future or a King Arthur past. But sensible people like ourselves can think of much better uses for time travel than that...

I mean, wouldn't you really rather know practical stuff like whether that handsome, conceited fellow in the next cubicle is going to lose his looks in middle age? And suppose you are late for work because you got stuck in a traffic jam. Can you travel back in time and, by cutting through the side streets, escape the jam? Then you could be sitting in your office, looking very competent, instead of sneaking past the boss's door, looking very guilty.

Actually, time travel is quite possible, but there are some strict limitations.

Time originated in the Big Bang, which happened less than 20 billion years ago. Scientists view it as a fourth dimension (length, width, depth, and time). But one astrophysicist has pointed out that in one sense, time is only half a dimension. For us, it operates in one direction only—forward.

Time travel into the future is no problem in principle. We do it every second we are alive. But can we travel into the future faster than other people and get there ahead of them? Yes, we can, but we would have to travel in space too, according to Einstein's relativity theory. Here's how it works: As objects approach the speed of light, time slows down for them, relative to observers who are at rest. So if you headed out on a really fast space ship, your time would run more slowly than the handsome, conceited fellow's time. Thus, from your perspective, you would not have to wait decades to find out if he had a bald head and a pot belly. He would already be middle-aged when you got back, but you wouldn't. However, if you travelled far enough and fast enough, everybody you ever knew would be dead and gone, so you wouldn't want to get too carried away by this travel-into-the-future thing.

In other words, time travel into the future does not mean that you can just pop into the future for a quick visit and then come back. What you are really doing is living at a significantly slower pace than the people you left behind. Their future will happen faster, in relation to yours.

The real problem for time travel is reversing the arrow of time and travelling back into the past. Relativity theory suggests that travel into the past might be possible if you could travel faster than light. If time slows down as you approach the speed of light, and disappears when you reach it, then if you went faster than light, you would also go backwards in time. However, in practice, the closer a body approaches to the speed of light, the greater its mass, and the more energy it requires to go faster. So while you could succeed in theory, you might fail in practice.

But what about the sheer paradox of travelling backwards in time? The famous conundrum is this: If you went back and killed your grandmother, you wouldn't exist. And if you never existed, you couldn't have gone back and killed your grandmother. But here's an even crazier paradox explained by physicist Paul Davies: You travel into the future and discover that a scientist has published a new solution to relativity theory. You travel back into the past and look up the scientist while she is just a brainy frosh and tell her the solution. Years later, she duly publishes it. But under the circumstances, who invented the solution? She didn't, and you didn't either. Did anybody? If not, how did it ever exist?

Paradoxes like these lead many physicists to conclude that time travel into the past is unlikely. Too much instability would occur in the physical universe if many particles started reversing their arrow of time. Things would get so severely messed at a fundamental level that the least of our worries would be who really wrote that paper!

For an entertaining look at the whole subject, try Paul Davies' *About Time* (Simon and Schuster, 1995). Meanwhile, consider Ecclesiastes 3:11 (NIV): "He has made everything beautiful in its time. He has also set eternity in the hearts of men; yet they cannot fathom what God has done from beginning to end."

37 Are Women Smarter than Men?

The main advantage that a larger brain size gives to men is for visual and spatial tasks such as parallel parking a car without losing a tail light.

Are women smarter than men? This is an important subject, and the biblical evidence is not reassuring for men.

St. Peter points out that Sarah called her husband Abraham "Master," to acknowledge his authority (1 Peter 3:6). The saint, of course, urged Christian wives to do the same. But he neglects to mention that, when dealing with her infertility, Sarah ignored Abraham and God and did exactly what she wanted to do (and thereby caused immense trouble). In the same way, her daughter-in-law Rebekah schemed to make her clever son Jacob Isaac's heir, in opposition to tradition and her husband's intention. But, in fairness, she knew that the older son Esau was not cut out for the job. Then Jacob's own wives, Rachel and Leah, dominated his life during their domestic war for supremacy through the birth of sons, with mixed results.

Although women were supposed to be subordinate in the Old

Testament, the biblical evidence suggests that most of them acquiesced in public and domineered or fooled their husbands, fathers, and fathers-in-law shamelessly in private, creating the impression that they were smarter than the men.

Is there any scientific information about the relative intelligence of women vs. men? Well, there is more than there used to be, because of new brain imaging methods. Here are some of the latest findings:

Head size is statistically closely related to intelligence. And men's heads are bigger than women's. Even when a man and a woman have the same body size, the man's brain is bigger. So men should be smarter than women—but on intelligence tests they are not.

Researchers at the University of Pennsylvania Medical Center published brain research this year that sheds light on the conundrum: Women have a higher proportion of gray matter, the brain tissue that makes you able to think, to cranial volume than men. However, the men have more white matter, the brain tissue that sends messages to other parts of the brain. This finding may explain why women do better on verbal tasks and men do better on spatial tasks.

Other evidence suggests that the main advantage that a larger brain size gives to men is for visual and spatial tasks such as map-reading, remembering positions of numbers, left-right discrimination, and parallel parking a car without losing a tail light.

Another finding just out this year from the University of Buffalo is that when men speak about difficult subjects, they rely heavily on the left (rational) hemisphere of the brain to process their thoughts. But when women perform the same complex task they use the right (intuitional) hemisphere equally with the left. Maybe this information will help men and women understand each other better in crises?

All these findings are presented with caution because the human brain is incomprehensibly complex. Most functions remain largely unknown. A lot of research sheds only a little light.

Christian psychologists used to stereotype women as being "good with feelings" and men as being "good with facts," in a way that suggested that the women had lesser intelligence. This belief supported a theology that subordinated women to men in a society that considered "facts" more important than "feelings." But it probably harmed both genders to be typecast in this way, and new opportunities for women are rapidly exploding the myths.

Last Saturday I watched, misty-eyed, as my younger daughter Cindy, who is very good with feelings, graduated from the University of Waterloo as a systems engineer, complete with the "Iron Ring." About half of her class are women. And, yes, they can do hard math problems and parallel park a car. They can even put prefab bookcases together at least as well as their male counterparts...if that is any cause for confidence.

The valedictorian urged the young engineers to tackle the two huge problems our planet faces right now: radical human misery and environmental destruction. I hope and pray that they take up his challenge. Most of the problems we face today need a practical solution, not just reassuring words about faith and hope.

But we need both sexes to be involved with these practical solutions to our world's problems. I am reminded of St. Paul's words more than ever, "There is neither Jew nor Greek, slave nor free, male nor female, for you are all one in Christ Jesus." (Galatians 3:28, NIV)

38 Recovered Memory: True or False?

Human memory is "wetware," a living document that is constantly rewritten and edited as we travel through life.

When the Christian and Missionary Alliance investigated the Mamou boarding school abuse scandal, the investigators banned evidence generated from "recovered memory"—memories that emerge only during therapy. The Alliance insisted on "continuous" memory that is, the memories people can always remember having.

Was the CMA right to ban recovered memory evidence? Based

on research findings, I think they were. But let me explain why I think so, starting with the question of "What is memory?"

Research on human memory has always been very difficult for a simple reason: the human brain consists of about 100 billion neurons. By contrast, an "artificial intelligence" computer network typically has about 1000 "neurons"). So research into what really happens when we remember or forget is bedevilled by the staggering complexity of our millions of interlinked living systems.

However, researchers have discovered the basic way in which memory works by studying the humble sea slug. The slug (Aplysia californica) is blessed with a brain that contains only 20,000 neurons, a low enough number for realistic study. Scientists made a habit of touching the snails' breathing apparatus (a syphon) and then shocking their tails. After a while, the slugs decamped when their syphons were touched. The researchers were able to show that new nerve communications had grown between the "Syphon Management" area and the "Tail Management" area in the slugs' brains. That explained how these creatures, who are hardly very well endowed intellectually, knew when to flee.

Human memory is vastly more complex but the basic idea is the same. A memory must alter some system in your brain in order to exist—and must alter it permanently in order to persist.

There are two basic problems with the idea of recovered memories: The account of how they occur does not accord well with available research on how human memory actually works. Second, while some proponents of recovered memory claim that "memories" cannot be artificially planted, research evidence shows that they can be and are.

First, research into the nature of memories suggests that an episode in our past is not stored in an organized sequence like a videocam movie but rather in widely scattered areas of the brain, depending on the type of sensation remembered.

Put another way: If you are old enough to be reading this column, what you think you remember of your early childhood is probably a reconstruction based on what you presently know as well as on actual memories. That is because you now have access to much information about that period in your family's and community's life that enables you to interpret what you experienced then. Your interpretation alters and edits what you remember.

Let us say that "Mommy's union went on strike at the hospital" when you were four years old. What that meant to you back then included very little detailed information about the workplace or family finances or exactly why Mommy was at home a lot, and shouted at you. What you subsequently recall of the event when you are 10 or 16, and perhaps when you are 44 and 64, will probably involve an expanding awareness of how it affected your family and a lessening awareness of what it really felt like when you were four years old. You are ruined for that. You have too much information.

For this reason, scientific memory researchers find extremely detailed childhood memories suspicious. They suspect that editing or suggestion is involved. Or, in the case of a severe trauma like child sex abuse, "dissociation" may occur. In that case, the person does remember, but intentionally stores the information separately from the rest of life's information in order to avoid pain. However, if the painful memory is confronted, it would be a typical confused and confusing childhood memory, not a detailed account such as a reporter might write.

Can memories be planted? Well, according to Elizabeth Loftus, writing in *Scientific American* (September 1997), her research team has done just that many times over the last 25 years. In one study, 25 percent of research subjects were persuaded to "remember" traumatic childhood events that never happened. Other research showed that 20 to 25 percent of participants would "recall" an event that never took place if researchers suggested that it had. And the more participants in memory studies are encouraged to imagine an event, the more some of them believe that it happened to them.

None of this proves that things long forgotten have never happened. Rather, it shows why independent, external corroboration is needed in any situation where accusations are made. Human memory is "wetware," a living document that is constantly rewritten and edited as we travel through life.

39   Is There Evidence that Faith Helps Cure Illness?

The grace of God is, by its very nature, impossible to study. God cannot be compelled or controlled by human desires.

At one time, many clever people believed that faith healing must be a sham or "wishful thinking." Through much of this century, to borrow British writer Arthur Koestler's phrase, the human being was thought to be "the ghost in the machine." The mind (ghost) and the body (machine) had nothing to do with each other. The ill mind was dealt with in terms of abstract (and largely untested) Freudian theory and the ill body was dealt with in terms of cold, terrifying, and often unsuccessful, hospital technology.

Nowhere was this tendency more evident than in the treatment of the dying. When Dr. Elisabeth Kubler-Ross started her work in Chicago in the 1960s, one hospital would not even admit that it had patients who were dying. But then how could it? In its own terms, it had nothing to offer them.

Today, of course, such attitudes have undergone an immense change. Even secular sources emphasize the practical importance of mental attitude in good health. And they are willing to concede that death does not mean that life is meaningless but is rather a challenge to make the best use of the time we have.

What is not so well recognized is that faith is an important predictor of good health. For example, consider some recent findings: One study in the *Journal of Religion and Health* found that religious seniors had higher self-esteem, which is important for avoiding depression (*Journal of Gerontology: Psychological Sciences*, 1995); religious heart transplant patients did better (1995); a *Journal for the Scientific Study of Religion* article found that church attenders have larger social support networks, which is important if you get sick (1996); religious nursing home residents are less likely to be depressed (*Journal of Psychology*, 1996); Duke University Medical Center researchers found that elderly church attenders had healthier immune systems (1997); and Yale researchers found that religious AIDS patients had less fear of death and better coping (1998).

There are probably a number of reasons why faith helps people to be healthier and happier. At minimum, Christian lifestyles forbid self-destructive behaviour (excessive drinking and smoking, extramarital sex, drug abuse, etc). A community of faith not only looks after its members but also encourages volunteerism, which keeps people alert and connected even when they are very old or ill. By contrast, many unchurched baby boomers will grow old in communities that do not care very much what happens to them as long as they are not in the way of whomever, in those days, is young and beautiful.

Still, we have to be careful about assuming that research of the kind cited above can vindicate Christian faith. Although a sensible lifestyle and a caring community are important, they do not really go to the heart of the Christian faith. As the Book of Proverbs makes clear, the benefits outlined in these studies are available to any community in the world that cares to live wisely and righteously. Nor are they the same thing as the individual acts of the healing grace of God which we read about in the *New Testament*, and sometimes see or hear about even today.

The grace of God is, by its very nature, impossible to study. God cannot be compelled or controlled by human desires. His grace, in particular, is always an intangible factor. Hence, people who want systematic proof of God's grace will probably look and look but never see it, and listen and listen but never hear it. Then— we all know the story—some sorry wretch at death's door is suddenly healed and converted. And no one who could write a thesis about it is anywhere about. For one thing, the respectable, educated person who could write the thesis wouldn't hang around in such a grungy, dead-end place anyway. That person would be studying on a clean, well-lighted campus (somewhere else). Oh well. The wind blows where it wills.

To view more information about studies on faith and health, go to the National Center for Healthcare Research site at www.nihr.org

40 Faith and Healing: Why Research Fails to Answer Many Questions

If the content of faith is ignored, statistical research is unimpressive.

The latest round of research into faith and healing has produced new findings and opinions, but no real breakthroughs. I think I now know at least two reasons why:

First, who will sponsor the research? Early in 1999, a team of Columbia University scientists warned against spiritual and religious practices in medicine, claiming that studies that claim to show benefits are weak and inconsistent. After reviewing hundreds of studies, they noted that they often involve few subjects and do not consider other factors that could explain findings, like age, health status, and behavior. They also worried that some doctors might use faith issues inappropriately.

These objections don't really add much to the discussion because they fail to confront the major problem lucidly explained to me by a doctor: proper research is expensive. It gets done if the sponsor benefits financially. As a result, research that might show that religious faith—or natural food, for that matter—improves people's health is unlikely to be funded, because no one can bottle and brand these items. Not surprisingly, therefore, most research into faith and healing involves few subjects and lacks other expensive controls. But of course, few of the critics call for properly funded research that would clarify the issues. Despite an explosion of public interest that they themselves acknowledge, they just want the whole thing to go away. Fat chance.

Then, in October, a study done at the Mid America Heart Institute in Kansas City, Missouri, claimed that prayer helps heart patients. According to heart researcher William S. Harris, patients who had someone praying for them had 10 percent fewer complications, even though they didn't know about the prayer. However, said Dr. Herbert Benson, a professor of medicine at Harvard Medical School, the study tallied complications using the researchers' own scoring system, which has not been demonstrated to be medically valid. Benson noted that research has shown that people who believe in God or prayer generally do better than those who don't. But whether prayer itself matters is unproven, he said.

What to make of all this? Well, let's hope that next time out, Dr. Harris uses a standard scoring system and gets someone else to evaluate his results.

But my second objection is that people routinely fail to distinguish between different concepts and experiences, all of which may be called "prayer" or "faith."

For example, some people believe that God wants them to be perfectly well either in this world or the next and that illness is a preordained time of testing from which they will emerge victorious. Their faith supports them, no matter what their diagnosis or prognosis. My hunch is that these people probably are more well than others at any stage of illness, and that they enjoy a higher quality of life throughout.

But some religious people feel that illness is a sign of failure. Perhaps God is punishing them for their sins? A relapse or worsening condition suggests that they continue in sin—and perhaps they are not really saved. Thus, faith, as they define it, would depress anybody and will likely degenerate into superstition. Who would be surprised if these people did worse than others?

A third group of believers might see illness and death as an escape from a world grown intolerable. They would not even regard a faith that prolongs life as a blessing. At one time, this was a common point of view and it may have contributed to the short lifespans of some of our ancestors. (As in "he died of a broken heart.")

All these groups might attend church and pray tenaciously. But if you ignore the content and conflate the statistics, a meaningless "average" of the effects of faith will result.

However, conflation of statistics is likely because the reductionist nature of most Western science means that the content of faith cannot, in principle, be taken seriously. We will likely be told that content is "too hard to measure," although one would think that a questionnaire followed by an interview would be a good start.

Anyway, if we really want to know more about the relationship between faith and healing, we will need research into the content of faith, not just the admission of faith.

41   Faith and Science: Cracking the Bible Code Controversy, Part I

Dismissing is not the same thing as disproving. If there really is a secret code hidden in the Bible, hadn't we better find it?

Is there really a secret code hidden in the Bible, one that you can access by counting Hebrew letters forwards or backwards at various intervals?

For centuries, Christians and Jews have sought secret messages in the Bible but no one took the interesting coincidences that some people found there very seriously. However, a number of books and seminars have appeared in recent years, arguing from various perspectives that there is a Bible code and that it is proof both of God's existence and the Bible's veracity. Only a divine mind, the argument runs, could embody a complex code in the text of the Bible.

The controversy received a boost in 1994 when three Jewish mathematicians, Eliyahu Rips, Doron Witztum, and Yoav Rosenberg, published articles in scholarly statistics journals on their discovery of the birth and death dates of great rabbis encoded in the Torah (first five books of the Bible).[3] Their work was taken seriously by professional mathematicians, though many disputed their findings and interpretations.

Meanwhile, orthodox Jews (Harold Gans), messianic Jews (Yacov Rambsel, author of *His Name is Jesus*), and evangelical Christians (Grant R. Jeffrey, *The Mysterious Bible Codes*) have claimed in recent years to find messages from God encoded in the Hebrew Bible.

Even non-believers have been getting into the act. Journalist Michael Drosnin, whose *The Bible Code* made number three on the *New York Times* best seller list in 1997, apparently believes that space aliens wrote the Bible code.

Yes, it's tempting to dismiss all this Bible code stuff as occult nonsense. But dismissing is not the same thing as disproving. If there really is a secret code hidden in the Bible, hadn't we better find it? Maybe it would settle theological issues that have bedeviled us for centuries.

But can we know for sure whether there is a Bible code? Yes, says Randall Ingermanson, a California physicist and author of *Who Wrote the Bible Code?* (Waterbrook Press, Colorado Springs, 1999). He claims to have found the answer, using the relatively new science of information theory.

Information theory, which owes a lot to computer research after World War II, enables you to discover whether a document is meaningful or just a random series of letters, even if you do not know the language. You can also discover whether a secret code is hidden in the document.

But, Ingermanson cautions, in order to frame the question we want to put to information theory correctly, we need to understand one of the glaring weaknesses of practically all Bible code research. The Bible coders typically engage in what scientists call "postdiction." That is, they go looking for interesting or acceptable messages, find something that pleases them, and announce their results.

Thus, where messianic Jews can find proof that Jesus is the Messiah, orthodox Jews can find proof that he is not. Others "postdict" all kinds of world events, such as the Holocaust and political assassinations. Interesting stuff, perhaps, but the signature of God? Or just a chance arrangements of letters that someone finds useful? After all, if you look long enough at anything, you see patterns...

Philosophers of science will tell you that a true scientific theory must be capable of predicting, rather than merely postdicting. That is, instead of merely going out to hunt for something interesting, you must state precisely what you expect to find, where, and why, all in advance.

Thus, Einstein's relativity theory received a major boost when astronomical events that the theory had predicted actually occurred. Notice that Einstein did not merely come out with a paper after the fact, saying "My theory explains this." He said, "If I am right, this is what you *will* see."

Prediction or predictive value, as scientists call it, forces a much more rigorous standard of argument than "postdiction" does, because the scientist is not allowed to select just any interesting result to bolster a theory, but only those that match the prediction.

It's actually a lot like the Biblical view of prophecy. The prophet's prediction had better happen, or else.

42 Faith and Science: Cracking the Bible Code Controversy, Part II

So, again, is there really a secret code hidden in the Bible, one that you can access by counting Hebrew letters forwards or backwards at various intervals? In my previous column, I promised to say more about Randall Ingermanson's book, *Who Wrote the Bible Code?* (Waterbrook Press, Colorado Springs, 1999). Dr. Ingermanson, a California physicist, uses computer-based information theory to check out the Bible code claim.

Now, it might at first seem surprising that a computer can be programmed to find a secret code hidden in a document written for human beings. But it is not really that surprising if you consider this: every human language has patterns that are meaningful within the language, but only over a short range. For example, in the English language, *t* is very commonly followed by *h*. And if you had to guess what the next letter is after *h*, you would be smart to say *e*. By contrast, *t* is only rarely followed by *m* (bitmap, nutmeg). So English is easy to spot over a short range because of patterns in the order of letters. So is Hebrew, although the patterns are obviously very different.

However, as Ingermanson notes, the short range order of language disappears over a long range. I bet you can't guess what the

200th letter in this column starting from the *e* at the end of this sentence is going to be. (You'd have to be psychic to guess that because you would have to know exactly what I am going to say and I did not know that myself when I wrote the *e*.)

So if a student wanted to take part of the text of, say, *The Lord of the Rings* and insert at every five hundredth letter, a secret message of her own to classmates ("The lecturer this afternoon is the dullest in history. Let's all cut the class and go canoeing in the Creek."), can a computer find her message? Yes, easily, just by checking for a high level of patterns (redundancy) at various equal distances in the text. No doubt the four occurrences of "the" in the above short message would spark the ol' bitmap into reporting some kind of pattern at the frequency of 500 letters. The actual text of *The Lord of the Rings* would not likely report any unusual pattern at that frequency.

The same test can be applied to the Bible, Ingermanson says. If there is a code embedded in the Hebrew Bible, it has to be spaced far enough apart that it does not interfere with the normal short range order of meaningful text. But if it is embedded over a long range, the computer should report a higher level of order at calculated distances, such as every 49th letter backwards, or every 57th forward. He has been unable to find any such consistent pattern. Hence, he believes that the patterns that Bible coders see are simply occasional pleasant coincidences that are meaningful to them.

The book is very interesting and easy to read, and it also summarizes the research of other writers on the subject. I certainly recommend it to those interested in a serious look at the Bible code claims. People who are interested in the "hard math" behind Ingermanson's work can also check out http://www.rsingermanson.com.

Incidentally, a statistical research team based mainly in the Hebrew University at Jerusalem has recently published the results of a test run on the Hebrew translation of Tolstoy's *War and Peace*, showing that the same sorts of apparent "codes" can be found there as are found in the Bible.

Here is my opinion for what it is worth: God's truths lie hidden in plain sight, not in any secret code. Far from it, in the Book of Proverbs we read that the lady Wisdom stands at the top of the street shouting, "Come here and learn some sense, before you get yourself in big trouble!" (my interpretation of Proverbs 1, 20-33). But we often don't come because we don't want to know the truth about our lives and what God must do to make them worthwhile. Personally, I find it hard to understand why God would bother with a secret code when he so often needs a megaphone, or even a brick, just to get our attention.

43 The Really Difficult Problems in Faith and Science

Far from thinking that the twentieth-century age of atheistic materialism has been hard for the church, I actually think that it has let us off too easily. Is God an Intelligent Designer or a Teddy Bear?

The Intelligent Design controversy—the idea that modern scientific discoveries prove that an Intelligent Designer created the universe—is fascinating. But what does it really prove?

St. Paul pointed out in his letter to the Romans that even the gentiles of his day could figure out that the universe was created by a Being greater than themselves. Realizing that fact did not make them good or even particularly knowledgeable or smart.

Today the world is emerging from a long night of bondage to murderous ideologies (communism, fascism, materialism). People are looking around and rediscovering the obvious: that the universe was created by a Being greater than ourselves, whose purposes we cannot always know. But that still doesn't make us very good, knowledgeable, or smart.

In fact, if anything, once an Intelligent Designer is accepted, we simply find ourselves back where we started. And if we are really lucky, we will know where we are for the first time. That means that we have to take up, once again, the really difficult questions. It won't be fun.

You see, the trouble is that, ideology aside, the really difficult faith and science issues do not turn on whether or not the universe shows intelligent design. Of course the universe shows intelligent design! The problem is—indeed, the problem has always been—how do we reconcile what we know of the universe with what the Christian faith teaches us about God?

Charles Darwin apparently lost his faith because of the routine evil that he saw built into the very fabric of nature. He particularly pointed to the fact that the Ichneumon wasp lays eggs in a caterpillar. The eggs slowly devour the caterpillar, which he thought a rather harsh fate, even for a destructive pest.

Personally, I do not share Darwin's specific concern because I honestly doubt that the caterpillar knows or cares. For that matter, do pigs sense their future ham-hood? Sentience (the ability to feel or know something) is what makes an animal's fate cruel, not simply the fact of eventual destruction. An immortal pig would not be intrinsically better than a mortal one, and a dead pig that does not reappear as a ham is a waste. But so many animals, innocent of good or evil, do experience actual suffering. Most northern ecologies depend on starvation as a major regulator of mammal life.

Robert Mann, Professor of Physics and Applied Mathematics at the University of Waterloo and a member of the Canadian Scientific Affiliation, rightly asks, "Where did sin come from? At some point in human evolution? If so, why is there so much suffering/death in the animal kingdom?"

Now, I am not saying that we don't have explanations based on our faith. I am only saying that any explanation is a tough sell. Suffering without apparent meaning is always a tough sell. And the suffering of wild animals who are innocent of good or evil and able to feel their suffering is a special and very difficult problem.

Far from thinking that the 20th-century age of atheistic materialism has been hard for the church, I actually think that it has let us off too easily. When people are not sure whether there is a God, they tend to let the church off the hook. They do not believe us anyway, and so they do not expect us to provide serious, truthful answers.

Provided churches preach a Teddy Bear God that people can believe in only when it suits them, they are benignly tolerated. The same way as you might hug your teddy bear when you feel like it but leave him in the attic for thirty years if you don't.

The trouble is, we have no mandate to preach a teddy bear gospel. And it is no use in the real, suffering world anyway. But the good news is that maybe a rediscovery of the fact of God will put us back on the narrow, thorny, uphill path that the Map says we should be on.

FIVE

Nature Is a Mirror— Interpret at Your Peril

This group of columns talks about the relationship between science and society, and provides a convenient place for some that were not written yet when I put together earlier sections of this book.

One common mistake we make in interpreting science events is that we think that science tells us how to see the world. In fact, we impose on the findings of science the philosophies we already have. There is nothing wrong with this as long as we understand that that is what we are doing and subject our philosophical beliefs to appropriate standards of judgement. What is wrong is to argue that we can't help having these beliefs because they are imposed on us by the world we really see.

For example, many august research bodies urge us to make use of live human embryos abandoned at fertility clinics in various forms of human experimentation. The view is, their parents, who have already conceived, do not want them. Why don't we use the unwanted embryos to develop medical treatments for people who *are* wanted? To disagree with this is to hinder the progress of science, we are told.

Actually, it has nothing to do with science. It is purely an ethical question whether we create a class of human entities that have no rights, as we appear to have done in Canada with unborn children, and now with embryos kept alive by fertility doctors. There is considerable evidence, as a matter of fact, that the stem cells needed for medical treatments can be obtained from umbilical cord blood as well as from embryos. But our society does not want to go in that direction. Having given up on the unique value of a human life, our society now sees endless possibilities for the use of those we do not value.

Incidentally, if you think that this can only happen to unborn children or embryos created in labs, have a look at the column on the fate of the Yanomami Indians of South America, whose wretched fate it was to stand in for anthropologists' delusions about "primitive humans" who were supposedly close to animals. Succumbing to some of the strongest human temptations—the love of money, consumer goods, and showing off—the Yanomami actually started to act like the anthropologists needed them to, and now their survival is endangered.

44 Nature is a Mirror—Concepts of Nature Tell Us About the Value Systems of a Society

People sometimes think that popular ideas of how nature works come from scientists. But that is not really the case. Popular ideas are developed by pundits to shore up social beliefs. The ideas are then used to interpret the findings of science.

The 21st century is widely touted as the century of biotechnology. To understand what that means, I recommend Jeremy Rifkin's book, *The Biotech Century* (Tarcher Putnam, New York, 1998 www.penguinputnam.com). Rifkin raises important questions, questions to which there have been few worthwhile answers. For example, he asks what it will mean to live in a world where agriculture is replaced by bio-industry producing cloned, interspecies creatures designed only to produce food. Where the escape of biotech creations may bring further environment havoc, and where our own gene pool is patented intellectual property controlled by a few life-sciences corporations?

For the most part, all one hears in response is the reassurance that 1) Top People are aware of these issues 2) but it is utterly essential to go ahead, and 3) anyway there is no turning back because if we did, we would fall behind. To that sort of shallow boosterism, Rifkin provides a sobering antidote.

I will not reproduce the information in Rifkin's book. Rather, I want to focus on one critical point that he addresses: people sometimes think that popular ideas of how nature works come from scientists. But that is not really the case. Popular ideas are developed by pundits to shore up social beliefs. The ideas are then used to interpret the findings of science. "Every major economic and social revolution in history has been accompanied by a new explanation of the creation of life and the workings of nature," Rifkin explains (p. 197).

For example, when I studied English literature over thirty years ago, I learned how medieval people viewed nature. Nature was viewed as a harmonious whole where the small things like the human body (microcosms) mirrored the great things like the planets (macrocosms). Class distinctions, subordination of women to men, the exalted position of the Queen, perhaps—all these rules were sanctioned by a sense of divine order that was reflected in the processes of nature itself. There was no concept of evolution or improvment. Rather, change meant decay and transitoriness (mutability), which were two of the evil results of the Fall. (Once you got past the Moon, however, there was no change or decay.)

Many scientific discoveries from the 17th through the 19th centuries demolished medieval thought. Darwin's theory of evolution (1857) had the biggest popular impact. But that was not primarily because the theory attempted a complete explanation of natural history. Its broad appeal lay chiefly in the fact that it explained the new capitalist society. People wondered why society had become so cutthroat all of a sudden. They were urged to wake up and realize that "survival of the fittest" and "me first" are the dominant principles of nature itself. So how could society be any different? We are really doing the right thing when we go along with our "selfish genes."

Today's society functions on capitalist social principles. It empowers women and lower social classes, because they are strong. But it poses a continuous threat to the existence of people who are weak, such as unborn children, the mentally unstable, or the very old. That is because anyone who cannot function as part of an interest group vying for power is doomed in such a society. And relationships of any kind become hard to sustain, because everyone's highest duty is the pursuit of their current desires.

Is today's social order really a truer reflection of nature than the medieval one? Of course not! In the infinite variety of nature, you can find almost anything you look for. Nature contains many examples of survival of the fittest, but many more examples of cooperation for survival, self-sacrifice, hierarchy, and survival by pure accident.

But when people look at nature, they pick out things they recognize. It is no accident that they recognize the things they already see in society. Thus, describing the face of nature becomes an exercise in looking in a vast mirror and describing the reflection of society in the background.

As corporations acquire the ability to make intentional modifications to your genes or unintentional ones to the natural environment, you can reasonably expect the popular picture of nature to evolve into one in which these activities seem as normal and acceptable as the ruthless pursuit of current desires does today. Rifkin suggests that the popular *Star Trek* series outlines the viewpoint that is gaining ground. More on that later.

45 Bans Alone Are No Answer to Land Mines

An estimated eighty million unexploded land mines are waiting to maim civilians in countries such as Angola, Mozambique, Cambodia, and Bosnia.

Christian aid organizations can provide plenty of material on that gruesome subject as they cope with children who, due to growth spurts, may need two or three surgical amputations after they lose a limb. At least thirty percent of land mine victims are children. Apparently, many of these children just disappear. In places where survival is a struggle even for the able-bodied, the land mine amputees are often "half people," viewed as valueless and burdensome in their societies, abandoned and destitute. Many will never come within sight of a modern prosthesis.

How bad is the problem? According to the International Committee of the Red Cross, one Cambodian in 384 and one Angolan in 334 is an amputee because of land mines. By comparison, the U.S. has one amputee per 22,000 people.

In case you run into someone who thinks that we bear no responsibility to Third World land mine amputees, you might mention that Canada exported land mines until 1987.

But the worst aspect of land mines is that there is no easy way to get rid of them. Passing political "bans" is certainly decent. But even if the bans worked, they would only prevent the problem from slowly getting worse.

Regular mines activate up to 100 years after planting. The mines cost between $3 and $15 to buy—a price that makes them available to just about anybody with a cause. The new plastic kind has made detection very difficult because traditional detection methods rely on metal parts. In the 64 affected nations, there is often no record of where the mines have been planted. Apart from the obvious consequences to those who lose limbs or eyesight, displaced farmers cannot cultivate or graze livestock on their infested land, so the mines lead to more hunger as well.

Thus, there is no simple technical solution just around the corner for what has been called "land mine pollution." Mine technology has advanced considerably since World War II but mine detection technology has not. Promising work has been done with radar, microwaves, lasers, and thermal neutron analysis. But all these efforts are at least five or ten years away from being a practical solution that uneducated people can afford and use.

Typical present-day methods include shuffling through the soil and poking a potential mine on a non-explosive side—slow, clumsy, and very dangerous work. Sniffing dogs are sometimes employed to check out soil samples from infested areas, but the scope of the problem is clearly beyond methods like these.

As Christians we ought to support the ban on anti-personnel land mines. But we can't just congratulate ourselves and go away.

We need to recognize that bans publicized by celebrities do not address the problem of the already buried mines. We must encourage the development of reliable detection technologies. This area of scientific research might advance more rapidly if more interest and funding were applied.

We also need to encourage the production of affordable prostheses for those who are already maimed. A child of 10 who loses a leg will need 25 prostheses if he lives to be 60. The materials cost alone is $50, a huge sum for someone who can probably only earn about $10 per month. And we're not talking about an electronic limb here, just an injection-moulded plastic part but better than a couple of sticks, perhaps.

Incidentally, the land mine problem certainly sheds an interesting light on the claim we sometimes hear that over the millennia, thanks to hygiene, education and general uplift, the world is becoming a nicer and more civilized place. As if original sin could just be scrubbed or lectured or uplifted out of existence...

46 Human Commodities

The grisly business of trafficking in fetal body parts may soon face Congressional hearings.

Pro-life members of Congress are pushing for hearings as early as this spring on the issue of trafficking in fetal body parts. The hearings, stemming from a voice vote last November, will study a little-known loophole that circumvents federal laws banning the commercial sale of human body parts.

The hearings may also shed light on a controversial part of the American abortion industry: the fate of second- and third-trimester premature infants who are aborted with their vital organs and limbs intact, allowing for use by biomedical researchers.

At the center of the allegations is the controversial Kelly, the pseudonym for a former employee of the Anatomic Gift Foundation (AGF), which is headquartered in Maryland with regional offices in Colorado and Arizona. The firm specializes in obtaining human organs and limbs for researchers across the United States. Kelly says her job, as on-site representative for AGF at an unidentified Planned Parenthood affiliate, was to dissect bodies, sometimes living, and ship the parts to researchers, usually under an innocuous name such as "biomedical specimens."

Kelly says she would get a daily list of the parts researchers wanted (eyes, livers, brains), and she understood that she was to procure the best, defect-free specimens. She says that each week she would see about 30 or 40 fetuses at around seven months' gestation and that several at various ages of gestation would be born alive. She alleges that a staff physician would kill any such newborn. Kelly claims that after an incident in early 1997 she developed profound misgivings about her work. A physician wanted her to dissect twins of five and one-half months who had just been aborted but were not yet dead. She immediately protested. In response, the physician poured sterile water over the infants to drown them.

Could Kelly's horrifying account be a hoax? Even staunch pro-life leaders are taking a cautious approach, especially because Mark Crutcher, president of Life Dynamics, the Denton, Texas-based pro-life group promoting Kelly's story refuses to make her available. Crutcher claims that Kelly would be in danger if her identity were disclosed publicly. Life Dynamics has produced a videotape of Kelly's story in which her voice is disguised and her back is to the camera.

Brenda Bardsley, one of AGF's founders, denies that AGF has done anything illegal and questions Kelly's credibility, according to *WorldNetDaily*, a Web-based conservative news service.

All of Kelly's allegations might be easily dismissible, except for one thing: after what she describes as a change of heart following the incident with the twins, Kelly provided Crutcher with protocols, or purchase orders, from medical researchers, dated 1988 through 1998.

Life Dynamics paid Kelly an undisclosed amount for her information, which included names and addresses of the researchers receiving the parts, and the age, condition, and state of freshness the researchers specified. Life Dynamics released these documents to the public last May. Doug Johnson, National Right to Life's legislative director, has not always agreed with Crutcher on pro-life strategies. But, Johnson says, "As far as what's there, it's authentic. Journalists have gone to interview some of the same individuals. None of them have denied, so far as I know, that these are authentic documents."

Concerning Kelly's allegations, apart from the documentary evidence she has supplied, Johnson says, "Everybody has to make up their own judgment about what she claims to have seen."

The release of the documents sparked greater interest among pro-life members of Congress in hearings. Senator Bob Smith (R-N.H.), an original author of the *Partial-Birth Abortion Ban Bill* in 1995, brought forward evidence last October that there is a successful trade in fetal body parts from abortions.

During a 1999 debate on partial-birth abortions, Smith read to his colleagues from a brochure that advertised the prices for body parts by type. Smith attempted but failed to enact a measure that would require reporting and disclosure of the trade in fetal body parts.

But in November, the House approved a "Sense of Congress" resolution sponsored by representatives Tom Tancredo (R-Colo.), Chris Smith (R-N.J.), and Joe Pitts (R-Pa.). That resolution asks the House to conduct hearings this year on "private companies that are involved in the trafficking of baby body parts," and to recommend legislative changes that would prevent such trafficking.

Diana DeGette, a Democrat from Denver, was among the few House members to speak out against the resolution. "We need to be mindful of the benefits that legal fetal tissue research has brought," she told fellow representatives. But she did note that if any illegal activity is occurring, the House Commerce Committee should investigate.

Rich Cizik, vice-president of Govern mental Affairs for the National Association of Evangelicals, says the Clinton administration has given its blessing to this use of fetal remains from abortions.

"The administration position at the NIH [National Institutes of Health] advisory committee level is that there ought to be [federal] funding of fetal-tissue research," Cizik says. "They lifted the ban. Abuse is something they should have anticipated. If they see nothing wrong in carving up human beings and selling their parts for profit, then nothing would embarrass them."

RELIABLE SOURCES?

Kelly is not the only valuable information source to be unavailable for questioning about trafficking in fetal body parts. Miles Jones, a pathologist and reportedly head of Opening Lines, a fetal-tissue procurement organization, has closed his operation in West Frankfort, Illinois, not far from St. Louis. Jones founded Opening Lines after breaking with AGF. He apparently pulled up stakes last September, after a local Illinois newspaper published an article about Opening Lines trafficking in fetal body parts.

Kelly and Miles Jones would have a good reason to avoid public scrutiny. What Kelly claims to have witnessed would, in some cases, be murder or manslaughter, says Sam Casey, executive director of the Christian Legal Society. "In the United States, even if an abortion is intended, if the child is alive and not dead, you've got to do everything you can to try to save that child," he says.

In addition, Life Dynamics itself has found a new spotlight on its controversial operations because of its reports about trafficking in fetal body parts. Crutcher seems to revel in his organization's outsider status.

"We don't make any bones about the fact that we are a very aggressive pro-life organization," Crutcher says. "We do things that some pro-life groups would find distasteful."

So far as *Christianity Today* can determine, Life Dynamics' strategies do not include violence, but the group does infiltrate abortion clinics. Crutcher defends the practice: "Some pro-life groups are going to find this distasteful, that we are working with people who are inside the industry. But then how are you ever going to know this stuff?"

The role of Planned Parenthood in the trafficking of fetal

body parts has also been subject to question.

Kelly says she was working at a Planned Parenthood affiliate. The affiliates perform only first-trimester abortions, a Planned Parenthood official told *CT*. Yet a number of affiliates state on their Web sites that their services include second-trimester abortions, from 14 weeks to 24 weeks.

OPENING A LOOPHOLE

American biomedical researchers began experiments as early as 1928 using fetal tissue to treat disease, according to American Life League, a pro-life organization. In 1988, Congress enacted a measure to outlaw the explicit sale of fetal tissue or organs.

In 1993, one of Bill Clinton's first official acts as president was to lift the ban on federal funding for fetal-tissue experimentation. The law itself, under the National Institutes of Health Revitalization Act of 1993, restates the ban on the overt sale of baby body parts. But the wording deftly allows "reasonable payments associated with the transportation, implantation, processing, preservation, quality control or storage of human fetal tissue." The act did not define "reasonable payments."

Thus, the actual bodies of aborted babies themselves are donated by the pregnant mothers and abortion clinics. An intermediary agency pays an "on-site" fee to the abortion clinic and processes the fetal tissue to order for its research clinics, which in turn pay a significant fee to the go-between.

For example, the Anatomic Gift Foundation assessed charges up to $280 for "gross dissections." Additional fees apply for "fine or special resections and fixation." Opening Lines offers much the same thing. One brochure from Opening Lines says, "We can provide you with the exact tissue to meet your needs. We obtain and maintain appropriate confidential consent and basic medical histories for fetal tissue donation." The federal government budgets millions of dollars annually for fetal-tissue research. For 1999, the NIH allocated $21 million for research grants and awards involving fetal tissue. Demand for fetal tissue has soared as a result of federal funding.

PARTIAL-BIRTH ABORTION

As information has become public concerning the use of fetal body parts in research, a new light has been shed on the practice of partial-birth abortion.

Since the controversial method depends on crushing the fetal skull, the remainder of the body is undamaged. According to the documents from Life Dynamics, protocols from researchers stipulate that organ retrieval must occur within 10 or 20 minutes after blood circulation stops. This requirement would seem to rule out fetal death by digoxin injection or saline induction because the fetal body is not delivered until hours after its death. Also, abortion by dismemberment within the uterus, another common method during the second trimester, would not meet the researchers' protocols.

But Life Dynamics' Kelly claims she witnessed the live delivery of a baby in an abortion clinic in which the pregnant woman's cervix was dilated sufficiently to allow the skull to pass through. She alleges that child was killed and dismembered.

Some analysts wonder whether the body parts trade explains the vigorous defense of partial-birth abortion by abortion businesses. That defense caught pro-life advocates by surprise and probably cost the abortion industry some public support.

"When I first heard about that procedure, my thinking was, 'They won't defend this, this is too ghastly,'" says Teresa Wagner, the Family Research Council's policy analyst for sanctity-of-life issues. "Well, they absolutely became offensive and unapologetic and defended this as a necessary medical practice."

Abortion advocates will soon have to defend partial-birth abortion before the Supreme Court. The court agreed in January to review the constitutionality of the ruling by which the U.S. Court of Appeals struck down Nebraska's ban on partial-birth abortions (*CT*, Dec. 6, 1999, p. 21).

Prolife sources believe that bans on partial-birth abortion can be upheld even under Roe v. Wade. Although President Clinton vetoed federal bans on partial-birth abortion in 1996 and 1997,

27 states have passed similar bans. Eight of those bans are in effect, despite vigorous legal challenges by the abortion industry.

REMAINING QUESTIONS

The House Commerce Committee, led by Tom Bliley (R-Va.), will have many questions to answer, including: How many abortion clinics and parts brokers are involved in the market for infant body parts? What is the role of researchers, including those receiving NIH funds?

Abortion activists say that late-term abortions usually occur in cases of severe congenital abnormality. But researchers who place orders for "normal donors" must know that many late-term abortions are unconnected to fetal deformity or illness.

Other issues have surfaced that only a thorough inquiry would answer: Do the researchers try to control abortion methods in order to ensure fresh specimens? Are women more likely to agree to abort if they are told that the body parts can be used to help medical research?

Many analysts have argued that pregnant women simply do not think about the fate of an aborted infant. But a 1995 Canadian study found that 17 percent of respondents, who said they would consider having an abortion if pregnant, agreed that they would be more likely to do so if the aborted fetus could be used in research.

According to Life Dynamics' Crutcher, Miles Jones says he is seeking markets for fetal body parts in Canada and Mexico.

Pro-life advocates fear that the escalating demands of researchers may lead to exploitation of the fetal body-parts market in the developing world. The pro-life members of Congress hope to start by securing evidence of what is really happening in all these areas as a basis for recommendations for legislative change.

Crutcher's ongoing refusal to produce Kelly is still disquieting to many pro-life advocates. But it has not so far deterred the House Commerce Committee, which has both a pile of documents to mull over and the power of subpoena, if needed.

LIMITED RESULTS

Despite support from the Clinton administration and biomedical researchers, fetal-tissue research has produced few useful results since 1993.

For instance, in Parkinson's Disease, long the premier disease in the use of tissue from abortions, few patients younger than 60 receive any benefits. Even the benefit to younger patients is often insignificant, accompanied by unexpected symptoms, such as involuntary facial twitching, according to the latest research. Still, researchers want more time and more fetal brain material.

In truth, there is no shortage of aborted babies. Pro-life activists point out that, whether fetuses are viable, dead, or dying, they are human enough to provide useful tissues for others. Why are the same fetuses not considered human enough to deserve protection?

Among pro-lifers searching for new avenues to stimulate public engagement on abortion, the most significant concern is whether the Congressional hearings will make a difference. "The possibilities for the administration to cover up what is going on are substantial," Cizik warns. The administration has pressed for publicly funded fetal research throughout the 1990s, maintaining that everything would proceed in an ethically acceptable manner.

Cizik is troubled that the issue may not be discussed fully in a Congressional hearing. He bases this concern on an incident from April 1998. During a briefing in the Roosevelt Room, President Clinton told evangelical leaders that his administration opposed legislation protecting religious freedom overseas because such a law would lead the "bowels of the bureaucracy" at the State Department to "fudge the facts" about religious persecution.

After observing six presidential administrations, Cizik says, this was the first time he had personally seen a sitting American president publicly admit that "our own civil servants will break the law if it suits their purposes."

So far, no one at the House Commerce Committee has talked precisely about what the committee plans. But Right to Life's Johnson thinks that House hearings into the trafficking of fetal body parts may help Americans understand some of the real costs of the current abortion situation. "I suspect that the majority of Americans, a substantial majority, would be repulsed by an order form that says I want this organ harvested within ten minutes."

Johnson compares it to the reported practice within China of executing prisoners according to the transplant organs needed. Cizik observes that the hearings "will reveal just how jaundiced we've become as a society to the taking of human life. "If the public yawns, then it will be evidence that we have indeed become inured to murder for profit. It is entirely plausible that the scales have been so tipped that nothing will outrage us anymore," Johnson says.

But with abortion on the agenda of the Supreme Court, Congress, and candidates in the November presidential election, the pro-life community has an unusual opening to spur the American public to rethink the view that abortion is a necessary evil and that fetal tissue from abortion merits respect, but not protection.

Conservative columnist Mona Charen wrote recently about trafficking in fetal bodies: "Some practical souls will probably swallow hard and insist that, well, if these babies are going to be aborted anyway, isn't it better that medical research should benefit?

"No. This isn't like voluntary organ donation. This reduces human beings to the level of commodities."

47 Embryo Research Contested

American pro-life groups, often associated with anti-abortion protests and crisis-pregnancy counseling, are intensifying their campaign against the use of human embryos in medical research.

In January, the Clinton administration began to form guidelines for federal funding of medical research that uses cells from discarded human embryos. The supply of excess embryos mostly comes from fertility clinics. In such research, the embryo is dissected and its stem cells cultivated. Stem cells develop into many varieties of human tissue. They are a critical component in the emerging field of regenerative medicine, which aims to use human cells to repair bone and tissue.

In 1995, Congress banned any research on human embryos, but scientists tapped private funds for research using aborted fetuses or with embryos donated by parents. Under proposed new guidelines, federal funds could be used to finance research on stem cells. Yet the federal money could not pay for isolating and developing the embryonic stem cells, which currently requires destroying a human embryo. Opponents strongly object to such guidelines, saying they evade the congressional ban on embryo research and that the proposed research depends on destroying human life.

REGENERATIVE MEDICINE

The goal for stem-cell research is to develop specialized cells, which could be transplanted into patients. For example, people with Parkinson's disease have lost cells that produce dopamine, needed for normal functioning of the central nervous system. Future treatments may include restoring dopamine-producing cells to Parkinson's patients.

In a major medical breakthrough, a researcher at the University of Wisconsin last November announced that he had isolated a line of stem cells using human embryos from the hospital fertility clinic. Although public money did not figure in the Wisconsin research, the matter sparked a congressional subcommittee hearing in December about whether the 1995 ban on public financing of research using live human embryos should be dropped.

Pro-life advocacy groups such as the National Right to Life Committee oppose the use of live human embryos in research. The pro-life organizations are not opposed to the possibility of stem-cell research. But they urge researchers to use stem cells obtained from umbilical cords or adults. Researchers are making progress in isolating stem-cells from adults, but it is proving to be difficult and costly.

NO LEGAL STANDING

In the United States, embryos kept alive outside the uterus have no independent legal status, and thus their fate remains in limbo.

But Nigel Cameron, professor of theology and culture and senior vice president at Trinity Evangelical Divinity School in Deerfield, Illinois, is skeptical of widely publicized claims that embryonic stem cell research must be allowed because it may generate cures for cancer, Alzheimer's disease, or Parkinson's disease. The research "can go in ten different directions or nowhere," he says.

Cameron is also concerned that the researchers will push the envelope by keeping the embryos alive and growing as long as possible for additional experimentation. "Plainly, once it is possible to maintain embryos in vitro for longer periods, there will of course be immense scientific interest in doing so because of the research possibilities."

The debate over research using embryonic stem cells is heavily influenced by the politics of abortion. The logic of the 1973 Roe v. Wade ruling by the U.S. Supreme Court means that many advocacy groups oppose protection for embryos outside the womb in principle, in case it impacts the right to abortion.

In most of Europe, by contrast, embryos outside the womb are not viewed as persons. But the Council of Europe's bioethics treaty protects embryos from non-beneficial research.

BIOTECH REVOLUTION

Efforts to restrain research on human embryos faces not only the abortion-rights lobby, but also the biotech industry and health charities that hope stem-cell research will lead to historic advances against crippling diseases.

Jeremy Rifkin, in his book *The Biotech Century: Harnessing the Gene and Remaking the World* (Putnam Publishing, 1998), predicts that scientific advances in human biology will force liberals and conservatives to rethink their positions on long-standing quarrels. Rifkin believes their common enemy will be a commercial eugenics industry in which both parents and society aim to weed out unhealthy or unwanted genes from humanity.

In 1995, Rifkin mobilized a broad array of liberal and conservative religious leaders to oppose corporate patents on life forms. The coalition was unsuccessful because the biotech lobby proved stronger and won the right to patent life, creating the possibility of patenting as well as manipulating human cellular tissue.

In the United States, legal protection against being patented begins at "birth," which would be precluded for human entities kept alive outside the womb.

Richard Land, president of the Southern Baptist Convention's Ethics and Religious Liberty Commission, commented recently on the issue. "Human cells, tissues, and organs should not be commodities to be bought and sold in a biotech slave market," Land said. "Some researchers have established in their own minds an arbitrary lesser moral status for human beings in their embryonic stage of development."

The Clinton administration's draft guidelines are meeting some resistance in Congress with 57 representatives going on record against them.

48   Human Embryo Research Resisted

A broad coalition of Christians is joining a campaign to resist efforts to weaken the federal ban on funding of medical research on human embryos.

A National Institutes of Health proposal would change regulations so that federal funds could be used for research with stem cells derived from human embryos. The regulations would permit the funding of research as long as the money to kill the embryos is not from federal sources.

"There are better, more promising avenues to follow in order to continue our fight against some of the diseases," said Sen. Sam Brownback (R-Kan.), describing the proposed research as "immoral, illegal, and unnecessary."

In July, 2000, the coalition released a comprehensive statement outlining its opposition to research using human embryos. The statement, "On Human Embryos and Stem Cell Research: An Appeal for Legally and Ethically Responsible Science and Public Policy" (www.stemcellresearch.org), was signed by 90 experts in law, science, medicine, and ethics.

The statement disputes recent claims that progress in stem-cell research requires the destruction of human embryos. Stem cells produce copies of damaged cells in order to repair body parts and systems. In recent years, scientists have isolated stem cells from human embryos and fetuses, umbilical cord blood, cadavers, and adult donors and used them to treat diseases. An estimated 100,000 live human embryos produced by in vitro fertilization have been left frozen in fertility clinics around the nation. The National Bioethics Advisory Commission is shortly expected to issue a final report, approving the use of the embryos to derive stem cells.

49 Film Industry More Fierce than the Yanomami Indians

There is no such thing as objectivity when people study other people.

Investigative journalist Patrick Tierney challenges 20th-century-style anthropology in *Darkness in El Dorado: How Scientists and Journalists Devastated the Amazon* (W.W. Norton, 2000).

In 1968, when anthropologists Napoleon Chagnon and James Neel visited the Yanomami, a remote Amazon tribe, measles broke out. The anthropologists claim they tried to prevent it by administering a vaccine; Tierney claims they might have intentionally caused the epidemic to see how Darwinian selection worked.

However caused, the epidemic was devastating. But worse was to follow. The anthropologists produced films like *The Feast, The Ax Fight*, and *The Fierce People* that cast the Yanomami as unusually violent. Anthropology students did not know that many of the people in the films died shortly afterward, not from ferocity but from diseases imported by outsiders.

In the media, the Yanomami were openly compared to animals ("baboon troops" in *Time Magazine*). The "primate" spin fit a popular 1960s sociobiology theory perfectly—in primitive societies, young men kill each other to obtain lots of wives, sire lots of offspring, and pass on superior genes.

What was the truth about the films? Well first, the violence was mostly staged. In *The Ax Fight*, a deadly offstage blow that chilled anthropology students was simulated by the filmmaker thumping a watermelon. And, as a missionary remarked to Tierney. "It's amazing how many alliances were created and villages were built just to satisfy the film crews."

That wasn't really surprising, because participating in films had in fact become a lucrative industry. Unfortunately, business competition also caused real fights, some serious.

And what was the truth about the Yanomami? The "fierce people" business was mostly a myth, Tierney found. The Yanomami had survived genocidal European conquests, plagues, and slavery by retreating to the inaccessible headwaters of the Orinoco. Traditionally, they had a relatively low homicide rate and preferred, understandably, to avoid outsiders.

Incidentally, polygamy was unusual. Because average life expectancy was only 21 years, most elders had several spouses, but serially. The polygamous men were generally well-off older guys who purchased a second wife at her birth. Those few young men who frequently killed would fit a police interpretation as "serial killers." They were typically rewarded by assassination, not marriage.

But the "fierce" reputation, promoted by anthropologists, has been disastrous for the Yanomami. Fearful settlers in their territories attack and kill them, and governments have justified breaking up their territories and giving them small reserves. Their numbers have been reduced from 20,000 in the late 1960s to about 10,000 now.

I believe that Tierney goes too far in his contention that the anthropologists intentionally caused the epidemic for research reasons. But their overall callousness towards the Yanomami in the interests of "objectivity" is repulsive, though sobering, reading.

Things haven't changed much, apparently. During the making of *Warriors of the Amazon* (1996) a woman and child who died of malaria were filmed. According to Tierney, they could have been flown out to a nursing station (a replacement camera was flown in from London), but that would not have provided the unforgettable drama of "primitive" death.

"This is by far the ugliest controversy in the history of anthropology," says Lesley Sponsel, a professor at the University of Hawaii who headed the American Anthropological Association's Human Rights Committee. It certainly dwarfs Derek Freeman's exposé of Margaret Mead's bogus claims about free love in Samoa (*Margaret Mead and Samoa: The Making and Unmaking of an Anthropological Myth*, 1983).

Of course, many anthropologists have attacked Tierney, just as they attacked Freeman. The trouble is, his research is exhaustive, and so much of what he meticulously describes is only too likely to be true.

The Yanomami exploitation and the Samoa hoax both illuminate a principle: There is no such thing as "objectivity" when people study other people. To report accurately and sensitively about other human beings requires truthfulness, fairness, courage, compassion, and insight. As good journalists know all too well, even to aspire to these qualities is the work of a lifetime.

People who claim that alleged objectivity can substitute for this arduous path are up to mischief. The dangerous part is, they generally do not realize that they are up to mischief. In the best case scenario, they try their stunt on sophisticated "primitive peoples" and get manipulated. At worst, the dreadful suffering they cause is not their own.

50 Use of Aborted Babies had Macabre Consequences

Adult donor cells work better.

In an AP press release in 1999, we were breathlessly informed that "stem-cell research tops '99 science. "Stem cells" meant a type of cell taken from aborted babies or from embryos abandoned at fertility clinics, once parents have conceived successfully with other embryos. This practice, we were told, "raises hopes of dazzling medical applications" because "such cells, taken from human embryos or fetuses, could be directed to grow replacements for ailing hearts, livers or other organs." It was Breakthrough of the Year, according to the editors of *Science*.

Now, stem cells can develop into a variety of different types of cells, which means that they may effectively treat many diseases. So a legend has grown up, promoted in the media, according to which stem cells from aborted babies are "no-name" cells that can be plugged in miraculously anywhere and fix anything. Their anonymous status perfectly suits the anonymity of the victims of abortion, doesn't it?—and, of course, the use of abortion victims in research lends support to the practice of abortion.

But what is the reality?

1) Stem cells are not exclusive to embryos or fetuses. Adults have stem cells too. (These cells may function as a "good" copy of your genetic code.)

2) Adult stem cells were more effective than cells from aborted babies in treating Parkinson's Disease because, according to a finding reported in the *Stroke Journal*, they moved to the areas where they were needed, whereas fetal cells did not. "We expect that stem cells will prove far safer and more flexible for repair of brain damage than primary fetal cells,"research leader Dr. Helen Hodges was quoted as saying. "They are not likely to worsen symptoms, as recently reported in elderly Parkinson patients."

3) The ideal stem-cell treatment would use the patient's own stem cells, to prevent rejection problems. The easiest place to find stem

cells is in the blood from the umbilical cord. A recent article in the *National Post* (April 5, 2001) told the story of a nine-month old infant who has lost an eye to cancer who will undergo a stem cell transplant from his own cord blood preserved at birth. With luck, this will save his other eye and his life.

4) The hunt for stem cells took a rather funny turn when teams of researchers discovered that adult fat removed during liposuction was an excellent source of stem cells for bones, muscles, cartilage—and of course more fat. Dr. Marc Hendricks, UCLA scientist and principal investigator at the University of California at Los Angeles, enthuses "Just as the Industrial Revolution transformed oil from trash to treasure, our research shows that unwanted human fat is actually a vigorous tissue with a tremendous amount of potential for good." (CBC News Web, posted April 10, 16:34:34, 2001) Okay, maybe. But we can be certain of one thing: Many people who hesitate to sign the organ donor form on their driver's licence will quickly agree to donate their beer gut to science.

5) But there is a macabre side to all this as well. What really happened to the Parkinson's patients who received cells from aborted fetuses as transplants? Writer Gina Kolata reported in the *New York Times* (March 8, 2001) that the research not only failed to show an overall benefit but also revealed a disastrous side effect: "In about 15 percent of patients, the cells apparently grew too well, churning out so much of a chemical that controls movement that the patients writhed and jerked uncontrollably."

An overdose of treatment drugs can also produce this effect, but there is an important difference: Drug use can be cut back. But there is no way to remove or power down the energetic transplanted cells. These results, reported today in *The New England Journal of Medicine* (April 8, 2001), are described as "a severe blow" to the idea of using fetal cells to treat Parkinson's disease, Alzheimer disease, and other neurological ailments.

Kolata writes perceptively, "The study indicates that the simple solution of injecting fetal cells into a patient's brain may not be enough to treat complex diseases involving nerve cells and connections that are poorly understood."

But surely the true source of the misunderstanding is the justification for abortion itself. All the abortion clinic is doing, we
are told, is getting rid of "unwanted no-name cells." It was a short
step to the myth of fetal cells as the answer to complex diseases
because they were not "really" human *and therefore were not subject
to the same iron laws of consequences.* That notion was perfectly captured in the breathless Breakthrough-of-the-Year press release. In
a real sense, the writhing Parkinson's patients were victims of the
abortion mentality too.

Endnotes

1   It is in fact possible to see some things inside a cell, including the nucleus and mitochondria, with a light microscope. But the very great complexity of the "molecular machinery" of a cell was not really seen until the use of the electron microscope. These microscopes began to be developed in the 1930s.

2   Strictly speaking, a clone is a very close match but not an identical twin. Most of the cell's genetical material is in the cell nucleus, which is used in cloning. Important genetic material is also found in minute structures called mitochondria, which are not copied over. However, for practical purposes, the clone is, and is intended to be, a twin.

3   Only one of these men, Eliyahu Rips, is an academic mathematician. Doron Witztum has a masters degree in physics and is a student of Talmud. Yoav Rosenberg, a graduate student in computer science, wrote the software.

Resources

Here are regularly updated sources of information, to follow up on key topics of interest. All these links worked as of mid-July 2001, and none required passwords or registration.

Reference Materials

Look up science information at
Refdesk.com
www.refdesk.com
Links to many reference sites, by type of subject.
Research-It!
http://WWW.ITOOLS.COM/research_it/
Another good bet.

Find science sites through
Search IQ
http://www.zdnet.com/searchiq/subjects/science/

Find recent science news at
Science Daily: Your Link to the Latest Research News
http://www.sciencedaily.com/index.htm

Ecology Issues

Find environment news, resources, and information
Environment Education on the Internet
http://eelink.net/ee_linkintroduction.html
Refdesk Environment and Nature
http://www.refdesk.com/nature.html, then your topic.

For a Christian perspective
AuSable Institute
http://cesc.montreat.edu/ceo/ASI/

Christian Farmers Federation of Ontario
http://www.christianfarmers.org/
Earthkeeping Alberta
http://www.web.net/~earthkpg/
Evangelical Environment Network
http://cesc.montreat.edu/ceo/EEN/EENusa.html

Origins of Universe Issues

Find arguments for the Intelligent Design position
Access Research Network
http://www.arn.org
Origins http://www.origins.org

Find arguments against the Intelligent Design position
Talk Origins http://www.talkorigins.org/

Check out outer space missions/discoveries
NASA http://www.jpl.nasa.gov/

Calculations and Information

Calculate basic math
MathType
http://www.mathgoodies.com/calculators/calculator.htm
Convert currency
NASDAQ
http://www.international.nasdaq.com/asp/GlobalCurrency.asp

Convert measurements
If you want to convert between Imperial and metric, use the convenient
calculator at
http://www.microimg.com/science/

Stop virus hoaxes
McAfee http://www.mcafee.com, go to virus library
Truth About Computer Virus Myths & Hoaxes
http://www.Vmyths.com/

(*Note:* Information about new links, better links, and dead links is welcome
at denyseolearyprojects@sympatico.ca, and will be included in subsequent
editions.)

Publication History

1   *Faith Today* July/August 1999. This article won the 2000 Canadian Church Press award for a third-person article published in 1999.

2   *ChristianWeek*, April 14, 1998. This column received an honourable mention at the 1999 Canadian Church Press Awards for publications in 1998.

3   *ChristianWeek*, August 26, 1997

4   *ChristianWeek Life*, August, 2000

5   *ChristianWeek*, February 3,1998

6   *ChristianWeek*, April 3, 2001

7   This review first appeared in *Catholic New Times*, November 2, 1997.

8   *ChristianWeek*, April13, 1999

9   *ChristianWeek*, May11, 1999

10   *ChristianWeek*, October 3, 2000

11   *ChristianWeek*, January 9, 2001

12   *Christianity Today*, December 6, 1999 Vol. 43, No. 14, p. 60

13   *ChristianWeek*, February 16,1999

14   This article first appeared in *Link &Visitor*, a Canadian Baptist women's magazine, in May-June, 1999.

15   *ChristianWeek*, March16, 1999

16   *ChristianWeek*, February, 2000

17   *ChristianWeek*, March, 2000

18   *ChristianWeek*, April, 2000

19   *Faith Today*, March-April,1999

20   *Christianity Today*, May 22, 2000

21   *ChristianWeek*, October 31, 2000

22   *ChristianWeek*, October 20, 1998

23   *ChristianWeek*, February 6, 2001

24   *ChristianWeek*, August 24, 1999

25   *ChristianWeek*, July14, 1998

26   *ChristianWeek*, August, 2000

27   *ChristianWeek*, August 25, 1998

28   *ChristianWeek*, November, 1999

29   *ChristianWeek*, September 5, 2000

30   *ChristianWeek*, December, 1999

31 *ChristianWeek*, January 19, 1999
32 *ChristianWeek*, June, 2000
33 *ChristianWeek*, May 29, 2001
34 *ChristianWeek*, May 12, 1998
35 *ChristianWeek*, December 15, 1998
36 *ChristianWeek*, June 8, 1999
37 *ChristianWeek*, July13, 1999
38 *ChristianWeek*, September 22, 1998
39 *ChristianWeek*, November 17, 1998
40 *ChristianWeek*, January, 2000
41 *ChristianWeek*, September, 1999
42 *ChristianWeek*, October, 1999
43 *ChristianWeek*, May, 2000
44 *ChristianWeek*, November 28, 2000
45 *ChristianWeek*, June 9, 1998
46 *Christianity Today*, March 6, 2000
47 *Christianity Today*, May 24, 1999
48 *Christianity Today*, August 9, 1999
49 *ChristianWeek*, March 6, 2001
50 *ChristianWeek*, July 3, 2001

Index

Relativity theory, 20-21, 123
Rifkin, Jeremy, 46-48, 141
    on terminator gene, 77, 78-79
Ritchie, Ian, 81
Ross, Hugh, 22-23
Rudd, Gene, 53-54

S
Science and faith issues, 118-20
Science fiction, 116-17
Scopes "monkey" trial, 105-7
Scorsone, Suzanne, 41, 43
Seed, Richard, 32-35
Selective reduction, 49-58
Shier, Patty, 49-51, 57
Shier, Scot, 49-51, 55, 57
Singh, Sadhu Sundar, 65
Smoot, George F., 109
Snowflakes, 57-58
Social Darwinism, 106
Sociobiology, 119
    Yanomami Indians, 157-59
Space, as curved, 20-21
Star Trek model of nature, 46-48
Stem cells, 160-62
    from abandoned embryos, 153-57

Summer for the Gods, 105-7
Superweed, 80-82
Surrogate motherhood, 37
Sussman, Gerald Jay, 47

T
Talesnick, Irwin, 13
Technology, 15, 62-63
Terminator gene, 75—80
Tierney, Patrick, 157-59
Time travel, 122-24
Transgenics, 29-30
Treaty on Bioethics, 43

U
Uncertainty principle, 20

United States, biotechnology, 42-44
Universe, as precisely designed, 18-19

V
van Donkersgoed, Elbert, 77, 78
Vander Zee, Delmar, 80, 81
Venter, J. Craig, 30-31
Veritas Christian Research Ministries, 56

W
Walkerton, 82-84
Water, 82-84
Wells, Jonathan, 112-14
Whole Shebang, The, 121
Wilkinson, Loren, 83
Winston, Robert, 33
Women's intelligence, 124-26

Y
Yanomami Indians, 157-60